How To Achieve
Your Dream Life:

*Start-up Advice
from a Successful Innkeeper*

Also By Michele VanOrt Cozzens

NONFICTION

I'm Living Your Dream Life:
The Story of a Northwoods Resort Owner
The Things I Wish I'd Said

FICTION

A Line Between Friends
It's Not Your Mother's Bridge Club
Irish Twins

How To Achieve
Your Dream Life:

*Start-up Advice
from a Successful Innkeeper*

Michele VanOrt Cozzens

McKenna Publishing Group
San Luis Obispo, California

How To Achieve Your Dream Life: Start-Up Advice from a Successful Innkeeper

McKenna Publishing Group
San Luis Obispo, California, USA

© 2012 by Michele VanOrt Cozzens

Printed in the United States of America

10 9 8 7 6 5 4 3 2

ISBN: 978-1-932172-62-1

LCCN: 2012940318

Cover and interior design by Leslie Parker

Visit us on the Web at: www.mckennapubgrp.com

For

Mike, Willow and Camille

Table of Contents

Got a million dollars? Looking to open a business that makes little money and creates endless amounts of work? Here's what you do…

Introduction:
Twenty Years Later

We fell asleep last night with the television flashing blue streaks into the room. I don't remember what we were watching. Hours later and deep into a dream—one of those dreams involving an improbable group of people collected from life's myriad of phases and set in a combination of every place I've ever lived—I awoke to the sound of an alarm.

It was a high-pitched noise coming from the TV.

Disappointed at leaving my friends behind in a dream that most likely will never recreate itself, I rubbed the sleep from my eyes, turned off the television and thought for a moment about how nice it was to see old friends. Then, I let go of the dream and faced the reality.

It was dark and chilly. In bed next to my husband of 22 years, the dog was burrowed deep into pillows against the headboard and her nasal-chihuahua breath interrupted the room's otherwise stark silence. Then I noticed the ceiling fan clicking at a low speed and the hum of the water cooler. I glanced at the blood-red figures of the digital clock across the room and calculated how much time was left before I had to get up and get to work.

In 2011? Work meant the initial chore of rousing the teenagers in adjacent bedrooms for another day of high school. I had one hour. One freakin' hour. A mother—especially a self-employed business owner in this economy—can do a lot of worrying in one freakin' hour.

It was November 1—a significant date in the Cozzens family. This is the date our business, Sandy Point Resort and Disc Golf Ranch, located in the Northwoods of Wisconsin, officially closes for the season. It normally means: Our docks are pulled in, the fall leaves of countless deciduous trees are picked up, and the plumber has been scheduled for the annual draining and winterizing chores.

As a seasonal panic stabbed my stomach, I fretted over whether or not we had managed to store enough nuts over the summer to last us through another long, cold winter. I wondered, will we make it to our twentieth season as Northwoods innkeepers? Will we continue to make this so-called dream life work?

When my publisher asked me to write a sequel to my 2002 memoir, *I'm Living Your Dream Life: The Story of a Northwoods Resort Owner*, he asked that it be more of a "how-to" book about the innkeeping/bed-and-breakfast industry rather than a memoir. Granted, the *Dream Life* book had a lot of how-to elements, however, it wasn't meant to be a how-to book. I just wanted to tell our story about *how* we went from being San Francisco Bay Area professionals to Wisconsin Northwoods resort owners.

Of the five books I've written—all published by McKenna Publishing Group—my understanding is that *I'm Living Your Dream Life* has been and continues to be the best seller. In the ten years since I wrote it, I have received empathetic letters from around the world from readers who are also in the innkeeping business, and grateful letters from those who were inspired to go into the industry after reading our story. Of course, there were also letters from readers who realized this business was not for them, and a couple critical reviews from those who felt the book was nothing but a lot of whining and complaining.

And then there were other readers who clearly resented our story—our success. One book review published on Amazon.com reads:

★★★☆☆ **We all should be so lucky.**, August 8, 2007

5 years living expenses saved and no profit for over 7 years... Should be titled yuppies buy a resort.

It's not much of a review, and I don't appreciate the "must-be-nice" attitude, not to mention the complete disregard for how hard we worked to make the business profitable. It does, however, address a key point that I definitely tried to convey:

If you want to become the owner of a bed-and-breakfast, a resort, or small inn, it takes cash. Lots of it. If you don't have the financial backing or wherewithal to first purchase a suitable property and then enough to sustain your family while the business is in start-up mode, this adventure simply won't work. You'll need to have either another job in addition to being an innkeeper, or possess a talent of some kind that earns you money.

So, with that very important caveat clearly spelled out, I'd like to take you on a how-to journey by relating our experiences as Northwoods Resort owners for the past twenty years. I do not profess to have all the answers, nor do I mean to suggest this business is for everyone. But it has turned out that the innkeeping business was the right choice for us. Understand, we didn't know for certain that we were cut out for it on the day we took over ownership of Sandy Point, however, because we had the brains and the backing, and the will to make it work, so far, we have succeeded.

Chapter 1:
Is This Business for You?

"You're living my dream life."

After hearing this statement again and again during our first few years as innkeepers, there was very little mental labor involved in titling my first book, *I'm Living Your Dream Life: The Story of a Northwoods Resort Owner.*

When reading this story about our "dream life," one may understand that while writing, my tongue was halfway inserted into my cheek. Anyone who sees the beautiful property on Squaw Lake that we are lucky enough to own and have as the place where we've raised our children can easily visualize the dream.

But there's a big difference between living at a resort vs. owning and operating that resort.

I believe the people who made the dream life comment didn't view me as the operator, only the owner. I don't think they even truly considered me. Instead, they looked at our property. This, of course, is why I was eager to tell our story. Our true story.

One of the first reviews of *I'm Living Your Dream Life*, published by the renowned, now deceased Northwoods journalist, Joyce Laabs, called it a "tell-all book." It was because I not only related the details about the ownership side of the innkeeping business, I also wrote about the actual job of being an owner/operator.

I covered both the dream *and* the nightmare.

The dream part is indeed centered around the beauty of the property and the ability to share it with others. The joy we receive from being surrounded by happy families reuniting each summer—hearing their laughter and accepting their praise for how well we maintain Sandy Point—definitely makes it all worth it. And there is no discounting the value of providing such an idyllic setting for raising our daughters.

In the *Dream Life* book, however, I didn't hold back about the more nightmarish aspects of this business, and the sometimes icky jobs of dealing with everything from stained bedding to cut toenails lodged in the carpeting. Nor did I gloss over the fact that the innkeeping business is like any other business that serves the public. The title for that chapter is: "People Can Be Jerks," and at this point, I need not say more on the subject.

At this point instead, I pose the number one question one must ask when considering whether or not the job of innkeeper is an option:

"Is the innkeeping business for me?"

Being an innkeeper is as much a job as it is a role, and the personality of the owners is the key ingredient to what makes an inn or small resort unique and inviting. Innkeeping not only requires a variety of skills, but it also requires certain personality traits. Keep in mind that skills may be learned; however, personality traits are more often than not inherited.

Consider this: When you sink your life savings into a property—whether or not it's an existing resort, inn or bed-and-breakfast—are you truly willing to share it with anyone else? By anyone else, I mean *anyone* who calls you on the phone, visits your website, drives down your driveway, knocks on your door, or walks right into your kitchen when you're not fully dressed. Old people, young people, beautiful people, ugly people; the wealthy, the cheapskates; fat or thin, tall or short, white, black, Hispanic, Asian, Native American, European; the deaf? Educated people, high school dropouts, the fashionable and stylish, or perhaps even people with breath so bad it could make the leaves on a birch tree wilt? Are you willing and able to treat these people not only as customers, but also as neighbors? Friends?

We bought an existing resort, which had been operated by a series of owners since the mid-1930s. In doing so, we inherited many guests, including a family who first came during the tenure of the original owners, Mr. and Mrs. Simon E. Anderson. This family, the Wilsons from Dixon, Illinois, have now made Sandy Point their vacation destination for four generations. They are lovely people, truly talented fishermen, and we are lucky to know them. When, for example, the senior Mrs. Wilson rings my bell and needs a special kitchen utensil, we'll more often than not also spend time talking about our families and sharing photos and stories with one another.

A majority—repeat—GREAT majority of our guests, both those we've inherited and those we've met during our tenure, who return each summer are truly delightful people. There's a woman named Ursula Zinger from Waukegan, Illinois, another guest we inherited from previous owners, who I adore. She comes each summer, escorted by her son, Joe, and she never fails to brighten the woods with her cherubic smile and her warm hug. We've watched her granddaughters grow up and we've said farewell to her beloved husband, Ed. I know her mailing address by heart from annual correspondence. There are many, many more I could name and it's difficult to include all of them, but, Juli, Beth, Joanie, Bonnie, Sherry, Carol, Chris and Tim . . . I treasure our annual visits.

Our resort also attracts family and friends. Mike's sister, Christine, for example, loves the Northwoods even more than we do. And one of my closest friends, Laura, who I've known since high school, has made Sandy Point her annual retreat for nearly as many years as we've owned it. Each makes us feel special and lucky to be in this role.

And then there are the not-so-delightful people. By this I mean people who have little respect for the property, or those who spend their time with us complaining mostly about things that are out of our control, like the weather, the fishing, or the bugs. The good news is that more often than not, these people do not elect to return. But that, of course, creates a vacancy open to absolutely anyone who contacts us when looking for a place to stay.

It's a gamble. (Gambol?)

In advance of our twentieth season as owners/operators of Sandy Point Resort, 73 percent of our bookings are by repeat guests. With repeat guests, whether they've stayed once, twice or fifteen times, they know what to expect from us and from the property. Clearly, they like us well enough to return and that's always a plus. More importantly, however, we know what to expect from them.

Overall, with repeat guests an innkeeper will know whether they are low-maintenance or high-maintenance. When reading their names in the guestbook, we ask: Do they typically show up early? Late? Do they leave the cabin in good condition? Do they leave behind a refrigerator full of perishable food? Do they have special needs of any kind?

When you know these traits and the answers to these questions in advance, you know how to prepare for their arrival, what it will be like when they're on property, and what may be required of you when they leave. Regardless, they are still individuals, and the variety of their personalities requires that you be flexible.

Let me put this in caps: INNKEEPERS MUST BE FLEXIBLE.

Repeat guests may have a basic understanding and respect for your rules and policies, but you simply can't expect every single guest to have complete and thorough knowledge of how you operate. If you have a short fuse or little tolerance for those who break the rules, you probably won't be happy as an innkeeper.

Frankly, I can't stand it when people ignore our policies or, in general, believe established rules don't apply to *them*. I have, however, come to expect this behavior and it now humors me more than it annoys me. The principal lesson I've learned in two decades of doing this job is that people will be people.

My biggest gripe used to be when guests showed up early, well before our check-in time. No matter how we tried to communicate that we don't allow early check-ins during the peak summer season—by telling guests on the phone during the reservation process, including it in our written confirmations, posting it on our website—some still manage to roll up in their big SUVs, trailer in tow, and a backseat full of frozen or perishable food, and demand entrance to their cabins. What they don't understand is that we have an established check-in time for a reason: The cabins simply aren't ready. Some people get mad and it sets the tone for their stay; however, most understand and apologize for being early. We invite them to enjoy some time at the lake or in the recreation house while waiting, and find a place to stash their ice cream until we're ready.

Remember, your primary job as an innkeeper is to provide a service for paying guests. And to be a good host, you have to greet your guests warmly, and like them enough to forgive them for being human. Trust, Mr. Chicago is just as angry at his son as you are for shooting a BB hole into the windshield of your boat. And Mrs. Milwaukee is mortified that she broke your coffee pot while washing it. If you know in advance that the affable long-time guests, Mr. and Mrs. Minneapolis, have a different idea about what passes for cleanup than you do, plan for it, deal with it, get over it.

New guests, or *newbies* as we affectionately refer to our first-timers, are completely unpredictable. It's possible to get a read on what they might be like when you're answering their initial inquiries and booking their reservations. Yet even someone who calls you eight times prior to arrival and poses twenty questions during each call may not be the high-maintenance sort you'd suspect. Some newbies actually listen to the answers and plan accordingly. Others, of course, neither listen nor read any paperwork supplied with the reservation confirmation. Further, they won't even look at you during check-in while you're explaining things like office hours and where to find the firewood, only to ring your bell well after hours and ask, "what do we do for firewood?"

Expect anything. In fact, sometimes as a means of self-preservation, I suggest you expect the worst. This way, I guarantee you will spend most of your time being delighted and pleased with the guests that come into your life, rather than shocked and disheartened over their behavior.

The succinct way to sum up the subject of whether or not you have the personality to be an innkeeper is to determine if you are a "people person." If the answer is an honest "yes," the next step in considering this occupation is to move onto the skills department.

Chapter 2:
Roll Up Your Sleeves and Get Your Hands Dirty

The skills required of a successful innkeeper fall into two distinct categories: Office skills and maintenance skills. If you specifically aspire to run a bed-and-breakfast, add kitchen skills to the mix. Please note, since our operation does not include providing breakfast for our guests, I don't attempt to give advice on menu planning and serving. For this I recommend *How To Start and Operate Your Own Bed-and-Breakfast* by Martha Watson Murphy; Owl Books. This, by the way, doesn't mean that if you have your heart set on an old Victorian Inn and the romantic notion of owning a B-n-B, that you should stop reading. In fact, my opinion is you should read every book published about the innkeeping industry, and contact anyone you know with experience as an innkeeper.

For the record, I've lost count of the number of phone calls and emails I've received from aspiring innkeepers asking for advice. I take time with those who contact me because I believe it's for the good of the industry. And I think most of us are very happy to share our dream life stories with you no matter what kind of specific operation we have. We don't look at you as competition. We look at you as allies, cohorts, brothers and sisters in arms, and we want you to succeed.

Running a small resort or bed-and-breakfast doesn't require a business degree, nor does it require advanced technical skills. The job does, however, require you to compile a business plan, and have basic bookkeeping and marketing skills, as well as know-how of housekeeping/cleaning, appliance/utility upkeep, and landscaping skills.

Make no mistake, this is a business first, a lifestyle second. And as a business the goal is to make a profit. With this in mind, it is essential for an owner to not only live on property, but also to be the operator. Chances are you will spend a great deal of money on a property or a down payment, and especially if you have a monthly mortgage, you don't need to add to the overhead and headache of hiring staff to come in and do the work for you. This doesn't mean you should expect to always do everything and know everything in order to make your business successful. On occasion, you will need to hire outside help from specialists and professionals like master plumbers or contractors, for example, or attorneys and accountants. It's a smart business owner who knows when to call in the troops. Understand, however, the success of your business will depend on your desire *and* ability to operate it.

Expect to roll up your sleeves and get your hands dirty. Ladies, you can still go to the salon and pay for manicures, but trust, you'll soon learn they're a waste of money. Add manicures to the list of D.I.Y. (Do-It-Yourself) chores that are part of a successful innkeeper's job.

In the innkeeping industry, there are three levels of owner status. Working owners, semi-retired owners and income dependent owners.

We purchased Sandy Point Resort from a couple who were working owners. Both the husband and the wife also worked for the local school system, and with summers off, they ran the resort with the idea of supplementing their income. It was not a profitable operation during their tenure, however, and the Internal Revenue Service determined it to be a "hobby," rather than a business. Hobby-businesses don't qualify for the same tax write-offs as profitable businesses run from the home—although operators may be able to deduct business losses from their otherwise taxable income. Any business posting a loss on its annual tax return will wave a red flag to the I.R.S. and an audit may soon follow. And unless you like the idea of a highly motivated independent agent hired by the I.R.S. spending at least six months combing through every bill, receipt and paperwork transaction you've ever generated, I highly recommend avoiding posting a loss.

Another level of ownership is the semi-retired owner. This status is given to owners who have retired from previous long-term careers and instead of income coming from jobs outside the home, they have nest eggs, pensions and other benefits supplementing income in addition to what they earn as innkeepers.

The third category is "income dependent" ownership. This means owners rely solely on the income generated from cabin/room rentals to support themselves. Income dependent ownership is the category to which we aspired. But it took a while. In fact, it took years.

In spite of having professional careers that we left behind in San Francisco and the Bay Area, as a couple in our early thirties, pension plans were not part of our financial scenario. We intended to live on savings and other investments, but it was also necessary to seek other sources of income while in start-up mode. For example, like the owners from whom we purchased Sandy Point, my husband went to work for the local school system and drove a big, yellow school bus. It was an excellent way to get involved with the community and also to learn the many winding back roads of the Northwoods lake country.

This illustrates one of the key points you must understand if you've determined that this is the business for you—and it won't be the last time you read this: It takes hard work *and* it takes money.

It also takes research on many levels, and by reading this book, you're well on your way. But where are you going?

I tell the story in detail about how we ended up in Wisconsin in the *Dream Life* book. Briefly, it was at the suggestion of Mike's brother, Jeff, who had a fondness for the great Northwoods since the family spent summer vacations there in the 1950s and early 1960s. We therefore had emotional ties to the area, but no real family ties or reason to move there, other than it was an established, popular destination with a long and even colorful history as a vacation getaway.

There are a multitude of popular destinations throughout the United States and the world. Ask yourself where you like to go on vacation. Where do your friends and colleagues regularly go? How far are you willing to move to find your innkeeping property?

Wherever you decide to go, for the sake of your business success, please opt for a proven vacation destination. You may want to believe you can build a heavenly attraction in the middle of a cornfield just outside of a no-name town with no supporting commerce or transportation, but most likely, they will *not* come. Rule of thumb: if the area has a Chamber of Commerce, existing inns, resorts, restaurants and shops that cater to tourists, it may be a viable area in which to establish your business. The local Chambers of Commerce, Visitors Bureaus and the State Tourism Agency in Wisconsin, for example, had plenty of visitor statistics (dollars spent) readily available for our perusal in helping to put together a business plan.

Now about that business plan. Write it before you purchase the property. In fact, I recommend you begin the plan before you even start shopping—just to see what you can actually afford to buy. The essential first step is to compile a personal financial statement. A personal financial statement is a list of all of your assets and your liabilities. Assets are things you own, liabilities are things you owe. Assets minus liabilities determine your net worth. A financial statement will also help you decipher between assets and liabilities associated with your personal needs vs. those associated with your business venture.

By the way, if you do intend to obtain a commercial loan to acquire the property, the bank will require a financial statement as part of the business plan.

Overall, the business plan is used to show profitability potential as well as the projected return on investment. Independent investors (or venture capitalists) will also insist on reading a credible business plan.

There are books and how-to pamphlets on writing a business plan or proposal, and a sample business plan based on our operation is included. Note, twenty years ago when putting together our first business plan, as a guide I used a pamphlet from the company Arthur-Anderson, which was given to me by a woman on my softball team. Another valuable source in drawing up a business plan specifically for innkeepers is in the book, *So, You Want to Be An Innkeeper* by Mary E. Davies, et. al.

In addition to reading books and pamphlets, don't be afraid to ask your friends for advice or to share their expertise. And by all means, don't let the idea of writing a business plan intimidate you. Ultimately, it will be one of the easier jobs you have when embarking on the role of innkeeper, especially because it's based on numbers/statistics rather than personalities and the random unpredictability of things like lightening strikes and hurricanes.

But I'm getting ahead of myself. After determining your net worth, you must ask: *What can I afford to buy?*

The current global economic climate dictates much of what is presented here as feasible. Regardless, before shopping for the property you must determine a budget based on your net worth. Although property values have dropped significantly since 2008, they are still far greater than they were in 1992 when we purchased Sandy Point Resort. It's all relative, of course. If you're shopping now, you must understand the current climate. Don't lament over what it was and please don't try to predict what property values might become. Since your biggest initial expense as an innkeeper is the property itself, it's important that you do not pay too much.

If you have a boatload of cash either from an inheritance, a recent investment payoff, or if you were lucky enough to win the lottery, you fall in the one-tenth of one percent category of someone who can afford to buy a vacant property and build your facility from the ground-up. As you probably won't see a profit or even a return on your investment in your lifetime, I simply cannot recommend this option even to you.

Without question, the best approach is to buy an existing business. But be careful. Just because the business exists, it doesn't mean it's in excellent or even good condition. In most cases, inns and small resorts are not big-money-making businesses. Owners, particularly long-term owners, often can't afford the upkeep on old buildings. If you're looking at a teardown, add demolition and removal costs to your budget. If you're looking at buildings/units that need a significant amount of maintenance or updating, keep in mind a bare minimum kitchen or bathroom remodel will run about $25,000 each. With either scenario, it won't be much easier on your pocketbook than if you were to start from scratch.

View each property not only in terms of its physical structures and surroundings, but also as a property with income potential and income expansion opportunities. The value is not just measured in land. It's also measured in the success or prospective success of the business. Any good commercial real estate agent or appraiser will explain that there's a difference in valuating commercial real estate vs. residential real estate. But it's important that you know the difference going in.

We, of course, bought an existing resort, which held a "recreational" rather than "residential" zoning permit. It included five seasonal rental cabins and a year-round home for the owners, all of which were originally built in the 1930s. The owner's home had been newly renovated/enlarged, and aside from the acreage and lake frontage, it was probably the key selling point of the property. We knew we'd be comfortable living there while modernizing the quaint rental cabins—all of which needed attention. Since the five small cabins renting at the time for $400 per week for approximately 14 weeks per year did not at once appear to be an attractive property for our plan to become income dependent owners, we viewed it as more of a residential property rather than a commercial property and valued it as such. However, because it had immediate curb-appeal for the business we intended to create, and more expansion potential than any other property we had seen, we believed we could develop it into a successful commercial property.

Prior to our decision to buy Sandy Point, we looked at nine existing resorts in our chosen area—almost all of the same era—and Sandy Point was by far, in the best condition with the most feasible amount of land for our intended project of creating a professional disc golf course on site.

To give you an idea of what the original cabins were like, "quaint" is the nice, real-estate lingo word that might have described them. "Antiquated" is probably more appropriate. I'm not exactly sure when the original cabins at Sandy Point were first updated to include electricity, but I do know indoor plumbing became a reality in the 1950s. It wasn't until we took over the property in early 1993, however, that my husband installed additional electrical outlets in the cabins. None of them had a single grounded, three-prong outlet in order to accommodate modern conveniences such as a microwave oven.

In start-up mode, we made these cabins work for us by using a lot of paint, updating the furniture, décor, bed mattresses, bedding, cooking and eating utensils. But most of these cabins had physical/structural issues we didn't learn about until several seasons into our adventure. If we were to go back to the beginning and do it all over again, we would have hired our own building inspector rather than use the one provided for us.

When purchasing an existing property, I therefore suggest you don't rely solely on your real estate agent to gather details about any of the physical structures. Hire a reputable building inspector to thoroughly evaluate each building and each system (electrical, plumbing, septic), and figure this information into your offer. Please note, we did hire an inspector found by our agent, and even though he did point out a few flaws and incompletions, the whole process of examining six buildings plus the outbuildings resulted in little more than, "this place is really pretty."

All information gathered from your building inspector will be valuable material when estimating start-up costs for your more detailed business plan.

A note on realtors: Once you determine the geographic location of your new business venture, look for an agent who has had experience dealing with commercial properties in that area. If you can find an agent who specifically handles resort properties, you'll be making a wise choice. He or she will be able to help you on many levels by providing knowledge of the local market, information about the tourism industry and supporting associations.

So, next you must determine exactly how you intend to pay for this property. Do you have cash? Or will you need to apply for a loan? Most banks will require a down payment of at least 20 percent, and to qualify for a commercial loan, you'll need a cash reserve in addition. A cash reserve is generally ten percent of the amount you borrow.

Do you need to sell a property in order to obtain the down payment? If this is the case, you may put an offer on a commercial property contingent upon your sale, but don't expect the seller to take the property off the market.

Sandy Point had an existing offer on it when we swooped in with our cash offer. I believe the offer had been in place for over a year, and it was contingent on the buyer selling both a house and a business. The buyer had in place what's known as a "kick-out clause," which required the seller to give her 72 hours to come up with the financing to purchase Sandy Point before our offer would be accepted. Obviously, she couldn't make the deal so the resort became ours. The happy ending to this story is that this buyer ended up buying another resort on our lake a year or so later, and we have become friends and colleagues. But the moral of this story, of course, is to understand the importance of having your financing in place when you find the property you want to buy. The gem that will ultimately be the basis for your successful business will not be available indefinitely. Get to work on your business plan immediately, and you can then fill-in the details of the property you wish to buy once you find it.

Chapter 3:
Tips on Writing a Business Plan

In the first chapter I contend, "the personality of the owners is the key ingredient to what makes an inn or small resort unique and inviting." Your business plan is the primary conveyance of what the personality of your business will be. You may follow a template found in any number of guides, but you still must make it your own. This is your opportunity to work out exactly what you intend your business to be. More importantly, it will show you whether or not it's a lifestyle you can afford, and it will present potential investors with the feasibility of your venture.

Begin your business plan with a summary of your concept. Make it accurate yet succinct. Follow with a more detailed description of the business. Describe the type of inn or resort it is, where it is located, and include the services it provides. Also indicate the legal structure. Will it be a sole-proprietorship, a partnership, or a corporation? Next, include a description of the physical structure or structures.

Whether or not it is an existing innkeeping operation, include a history of the property. Keep in mind if you purchase a residential property with the intention of turning it into a commercial operation, you will need to consider zoning ordinances and zoning alteration procedures, which may be costly, time-consuming and, as we experienced firsthand with a property we eventually annexed to our resort, political.

To illustrate, in 1995 we opted to buy the five-acre property adjacent to Sandy Point Resort when our neighbors decided to move closer to town. Because acquisition of the property would not only add an additional 200 feet of lake frontage, but also add five acres and a sizeable rental unit, it was an attractive income expansion opportunity. Our plan was to annex it to the resort. The property, however, had a R-1 single-family residential zoning, which denied "transient lodging." Transient use allows rental of sleeping quarters or dwelling units for periods of less than one month. To make it part of our business, we had to change the zoning. We opted for a recreational zoning to correspond with the current zoning of Sandy Point Resort.

In our offer, we included the rezoning contingency, which obviously we needed in order to *legally* rent the lodge on a nightly or weekly basis. We thought it would be a simple process. It wasn't. When the public notice appeared in the newspaper indicating we sought a recreational zoning, someone took that to mean we planned to build a whole host of structures and attractions allowed in a recreational zone. Rumors arose about things like high-rise condos, an off-road racing track, even an airplane landing strip! One lake resident, who by the way, sold his home and moved away some ten years ago, drew up a petition warning neighbors to "Stop the Sandy Point Developers!" Many people signed it without even asking us our plans.

So, what we thought would be a simple process turned out to be a bit of a legal battle with multiple zoning hearings. The good news is that we won. Ultimately the Board understood we were only trying to adhere to proper zoning regulations. I'm certain that everyone who attended those hearings understood we weren't going to construct high-rise condos or airplane landing strips. Also, I dare say that nearly everyone knew a neighbor or two who *illegally* rented their lake homes and cottages as commercial property zoned with the restrictions allocated to a single-family status. I like to believe we were rewarded for doing the right thing.

The lesson here applies not only to understanding zoning issues, but also it's about the importance of the income expansion opportunities of any property you consider. Whether or not it's an existing inn or resort, it simply MUST have income expansion potential. This doesn't necessarily mean you must plan to acquire more property; however, you must have a plan for earning more income.

When compiling the history of the property, try to gather as much information as you can from the current owners, public real estate records, neighbors, newspaper archives, etc. Not every property is blessed with a rich, colorful or even documented history; however, finding out all you can about your intended new home will prove useful. Trust me, the majority of your future guests will ask. Mostly, they want to know about you, but also, they'll ask how you have come to own the property.

The question we hear most often is: "Did you grow up here and inherit this place?" Hopefully our children will be able to answer "yes" to this question, but chances are you, like us, will not.

Most of the history of Sandy Point Resort came to us by chance. The owners from whom we purchased it had only eight years experience; however, within the first five years of our operation, we had the pleasure of meeting nearly every owner—including in 1996, the relatives and descendants of Simon and Alma Anderson, the original property owners and builders of the resort. It was a momentous day when the Andersons, one elder and one middle-aged couple, came to the property. First of all, the elder couple were so feeble, they couldn't tour the grounds, and actually never went beyond our driveway. I remember with great clarity that they were beautiful people. Tall and thin, and as snow white as birch trees, they couldn't have been more charming.

Two weeks after their visit, we received the following letter:

August 14, 1996
Dear Mike and Michele of Sandy Point Resort:

In late July, we stopped at your resort and visited with Michele. There were four of us, my aunt and uncle, (the Lawrence Anderson's) and my husband and I. We were looking for the resort that my great aunt and uncle had built on Squaw Lake in the mid-1930's. You told us that yes, indeed, your resort was one of the two oldest on the lake, and was built around that time. We walked around and hoped that my aunt and uncle would find something that triggered their memories.

We think the resort that is now yours was built by Simon and Alma Anderson in the mid-30's. They had moved to Wisconsin after losing their farm near DeKalb, IL during the

Depression. All of my aunts and uncles spent their honeymoons there from 1939 to 1945. After we got home from our
vacation this year we all searched the old photo albums to
find pictures. I've had copies made of the best ones and am
sending them for you to enjoy. I hope you can confirm that
your resort is the same one built by Simon Anderson. Maybe
the position on the lakeshore or some features of the house
or cabin will make the definite connection.

No one in the family remembers the name Sandy Point.
Michele told us that she thought the resort had always been
called by that name. Perhaps the owners after the Andersons
used that name.

As you can see by the small pictures, it was very hard
work building the resort! Aunt Alma really got "down &
dirty!" She even washed her hair outside, probably with
rainwater. Uncle Simon died before Aunt Alma, and she
moved to a small cabin just a few miles from the resort until
her death.

I enjoyed the notes on the backs of the postcards so I
copied those also. The messages sent home from vacations
haven't changed much over the last 60 years.

Please let me know if you can confirm that your resort is
the same one in these pictures. (You can keep the pictures if
it is, please return them if not). All of the family is anxious
to know.

Sincerely,
Carolyn Lawrence
Avon, IL

The package was filled with black-and-white photos and copies
of postcards with fountain pen messages dating from the 1930s and
1940s. There was no mistaking the cabins and the shoreline. We con-

firmed that our resort was indeed the one for which they had been looking.

We also found original postcards, one with photos of cabins and the lakefront and a tag reading: "Simon E. Anderson, CAMP FIRE LODGE, Squaw Lake, Lac du Flambeau, Wis." and another with a photo of Simon and Alma in front of their house. Dated September 12, 1935, the one-cent cancelled stamp was from Minocqua, Wis. at 5:30 p.m. This postcard, addressed to Mrs. S.H. Larson in Detroit, Michigan had no zip code. It reads:

Dear folks,

This is where Phil and I landed for a visit. Smith's called and took us along to see Simon Anderson's new resort. Lovely place, beautiful country. Leaving today for home via another route. Grand sailing along the road. Plenty of boating and fishing here. Love Gerda.

We had a similar experience meeting former owners, Mr. and Mrs. Bickelhoff, who purchased the resort from the Andersons at some point after 1952. They named it Sandy Point, and their tenure lasted some twenty years. The Bickelhoff's son, Walt, had been delivering propane to our property since the day we moved in, but it took his parents a few years into our tenure to gather the courage to visit us. They still lived in the area, in fact, only a mile or two down the road, but they hadn't been back to Sandy Point since they sold it in the early 1970s. Unlike the Anderson family, they knew exactly where the resort was located.

The first thing Mrs. Bickelhoff commented on was the size and growth of the cedar trees they had planted along our current driveway, in an area we now call "Birdhouse Island." Secondly, she breathed a sigh of relief. "This isn't my home," she said while looking at our house, which we had expanded and updated even more than the owners from whom we had purchased the resort. My guess was Mrs. Bickelhoff didn't want to leave the resort back when they found it necessary to sell, and felt returning would be bittersweet. Either that, or she was so eager to get away, she vowed to never return! I can't say for certain.

A week after their visit, Walt delivered a collection of photos and postcards from their ownership era, which provided a thorough second chapter of the resort's history. It was from them that we learned the five original cabins had names beyond numbers one through five. And it led us to name two of the new cabins we built to replace the originals, "Hilltop" and "The Big House." One of the cabins, the smallest, which we knew as cabin #4, was originally called "Honeymoon." When we learned that all the relatives of the Andersons had spent their honeymoons at the resort, we didn't wonder why.

What we didn't learn about Sandy Point from the former owners, we made up. For example, there's an old car, a 1954 Pontiac, on the property, which is now a part of the unique ambience of the disc golf course. We discovered the rusted, bullet-hole ridden, overturned hunk-of-junk in the woods while cross country skiing during our first winter there. Soon we made it a part of what is now hole #22 on our disc golf course. Walt Bickelhoff informed us that the Pontiac once belonged to him, and he drove it into the woods one day and left it there to die. The bullet holes were from target practice.

Over the years we've had a lot of fun making up stories about the old car, telling our guests, for example, that it belonged to Al Capone. For those of you who may not know, Capone, the notorious gangster/bootlegger from Chicago, reportedly used the Northwoods as a hideout from law enforcement officials. The incredible stone and wood cabin, once owned—or allegedly owned—by Capone's family, sits on 407 acres just north of us on Blueberry Lake in Couderay, WI. (In 2009, the Chippewa Valley Bank purchased the property at auction for $2.6 million).

The Northwoods is famous for its gangster history. The 2009 film *Public Enemies*, starring Johnny Depp as gangster/bank robber John Dillinger, for example, was filmed in part at the Little Bohemia Lodge, in Manitowish Waters, WI. That film was the best thing to ever happen for the restaurant business at Little Bohemia, one of our local favorites, where original bullet holes from the 1934 shootout are preserved in walls and windows, and the wait staff now dresses as gangsters. The menu features entrees like the "Dillinger Medallions," and my favorite, the "Dillinger Signature Salad."

The point is, knowing the history of your property, either fully documented or of the more handcrafted, family-legend variety, will ultimately prove to be a sales tool and a valuable part of your business plan. I am not suggesting that you fabricate tall tales and present what are essentially lies as facts to potential investors, but I do believe you should use all the information you gather to your advantage, and to the end of making the property appear to be an attractive investment.

The next topic to cover in your business plan is marketing. The objective is to determine the sales potential of the property. In this section you will identify your customers as well as your competition. Ask the owners/sellers for this information, which will be specific and accurate (rather than estimated) to the property you intend to market. Hopefully, they'll have this data readily available, but don't count on it. You may be buying a property from someone who is not of the computer generation or is selling the business due in part to poor management or organizational skills. Nevertheless, in advance, before you find the property, research visitor statistics and occupancy rates in the geographic area or region, which are available from the local Chamber of Commerce or the State Tourism Office. If you do obtain records from the owner/seller, you can evaluate how the two sets of statistics compare to one another in order to get a realistic picture of your prospects.

Your marketing plan should further indicate how you intend to either become or remain competitive in that area. Outline how you propose to attract guests and/or maintain existing guests. Determine what role the ambience of the property will play, and include the pricing structure as well as the policies and procedures. What associations will you join and what types of referrals do you expect to obtain? What types of advertising will you invest in and/or what kind of publicity will you seek? Keep in mind that advertising costs money while publicity is free, but free publicity is not always simple to obtain. You may not get much more than an article in the local newspaper in thc "New Business" section. Also, don't discount the value of today's social networks, like Facebook and Twitter. We managed to reach 1,000 "likes" of our Sandy Point Resort Facebook page in just a few short months, and regularly use it to announce cancellations and/ or special events. And if you're not afraid to write, consider a blog. If the idea of writing makes you queasy, use it to post photos. Guests love to see photos of themselves hoisting a thirty-five pound musky caught in your lake. It's definitely good advertising.

Moving on to Personnel, include your professional resume. If you are working with a partner or spouse, and I recommend you do, include both resumes. If you want to market your property as "family-owned and operated," you don't need to include resumes of your children (unless it's appropriate and useful), but by all means, describe the types of work/chores in which the children will participate. It will only add to the charm of your family-owned operation.

We didn't have children when we purchased Sandy Point Resort, and for the first several years of their lives, trust they didn't help with the resort operation. On the contrary. It wasn't until they were in elementary school when they first started their weekly lemonade stand; however, this only made pocket change for *them*! It was years before they understood the concept of overhead and realized they had to purchase the lemonade and all the goodies they had previously swiped from our resort store from their "profits." Late in adolescence, they helped run the store, deliver messages and finally, they joined the housekeeping staff and have mastered, among other things, the art of making a "crisp" bed.

In the Personnel section, describe the specific jobs the property presents and how the workload will be handled. Include a chart of responsibilities, distributing the tasks of office work (bookkeeping and marketing) vs. property maintenance (building upkeep and landscaping); and public relations (hosting and guest services) vs. cleaning (cabin/room turnover and laundry).

Also include a list of professional consultants who are readily available (or hirable) to help you achieve your business goals. This list may consist of a general building contractor or architect, a master plumber or electrician, an insurance agent, attorney or accountant. It may also include an advertising agency, graphic designer, web master or printer. As much as you may want to or, for budgeting purposes, need to avoid hiring professionals to do jobs you may otherwise be qualified to do yourself, it's important to understand that for some projects, you will need help and you must account for it.

The final section of your business plan contains detailed financial information. It may be the last thing you present, but it's ultimately the most important and will take the most time. This is not a part of your business plan that should have any sort of fabrication to make it more attractive. Base it on real numbers. Granted, in some areas you will be forced to estimate; however, it's better to estimate expenses on the high side and income on the low side.

The business plan we first put together for Sandy Point Resort followed the expenses high/income low suggestion, and by crunching the numbers and estimating start-up costs, we expected it to be five years before we made a profit. We therefore knew going in that we'd have to find ways to supplement our income, burn a lot of savings and cash in on investments. This is a fact the business plan helped to establish for us. What it didn't foretell, however, was that it would actually take seven years before the business was profitable. We simply didn't account for the circumstances that were more difficult or even impossible to predict. Namely, things like lawsuits and zoning petitions, or paving roads and having babies. In some cases, we made the choice—or had the choice made for us—to increase our expenses. This is something that didn't end even after we became profitable. When in 2008, for example, something called a "microburst" hit our waterfront like an explosion, it turned our docks into kindling and threw all our boats some 100 feet, smashing them into nearby trees. We didn't have much of a choice but to have everything cleaned up *and* replaced. And in this case, we had to do it overnight since we expected a fresh crop of new guests to check in the next day. This, by the way, was only one of the devastating and damaging storms we have endured over the years. Another big one in August of 2000, which we named "The Perfect Storm," knocked out our electrical power for five days. It led to the purchase of five generators, which we now have "on call" and ready to go in the event of what has turned out to be frequent power outages.

I remember waking up one early June morning during 2008 and watching the morning news, which broadcasted footage of a lake draining in south-central Wisconsin. Lake Delton, a manmade lake near the Wisconsin Dells, was created in the late 1920s as a tourist attraction and resort area. Today some 20 resorts reside there and it's also the site of the famous Tommy Bartlett Waterski Show. Due to excessive rainfall and flooding in the area that spring, part of the dam built to create the lake crumbled under the pressure of the floods, and it caused the lake water to drain into the nearby Wisconsin River. The powerful flow took at least three houses with it, and all that was left once the lake water was gone were mud puddles. Naturally I felt awful for everyone who lived on that lake, especially the people who had completely lost their homes. And yet, mostly I felt for the resort owners. Who would show up for a lake vacation that summer when there was no lake outside their cabin? I wondered how on earth the resorts were going to make ends meet after a lost season? Yikes! What would happen to us if Squaw Lake were to suddenly disappear?

Don't be naïve when it comes to estimating for unpredictable circumstances, particularly when it comes to the forces of nature. For example, if your property is in a hurricane zone, there will eventually be a hurricane. If you're in the tornado belt, expect a twister. Earthquakes? Tropical Storms? Floods? Droughts? Fires? Yes, yes, yes, yes, and yes. Mother Nature happens, my friends, and she will happen to you. Plan for it. And plan for it in terms of dollars.

According to Mary E. Davis, the financial section of your business plan should include seven topics: "a summary of financial needs and your plans to meet them, your personal financial statement, the projected personal benefit income, projected occupancy rate, a cash-flow projection month-by-month, a balance sheet (if buying an existing inn) and a pro forma (estimate or projected profit/loss statement), and an itemization of start-up costs."[1]

In her book, *So, You Want To Be An Innkeeper*, Davis provides a useful template to compute your financial needs. Davis and her fellow authors also breakdown example costs of renovating and furnishings, standard expenses, and formulas for calculating projected occupancy rates and cash flow. I used this book like a bible when putting together the financial section of our business plan, and I suggest you do as well. The way I try to help you further is by providing some real figures based on 20 years of bookkeeping. In the financial information section of the business plan I present in the next chapter, I focus on projected occupancy rates—conservative estimates—and operational expenses—generous estimates. I do not cover start-up expenses, nor do I include information about our retail operation. It is up to you to come up with start-up figures based on the property you intend to purchase. Additionally, I highly recommend that you use these figures and the figures you come up with to go a step further, and illustrate projected income for three to five years.

[1] *So, You Want To Be An Innkeeper: The Definitive Guide to Operating a Successful Bed-and-Breakfast or Country Inn*, Mary E. Davis, Pat Hardy, Jo Ann M. Bell, Susan Brown. Chronicle Books, 3rd Rev. Ed., 1996.

Our books are completely computerized and the bookkeeping program I use is called AccountEdge. Note, the original program was M.Y.O.B (Managing Your Own Business); but just as I continued upgrading computers and operating systems, so evolved the compatibility of the bookkeeping program. It is a sophisticated, complete system, enabling users to generate balance sheets, profit and loss statements, and any number of account reports. I also use it to manage our business checking account.

Bookkeeping chores are my single most important contribution to managing the business, and when I decided to become an innkeeper, my bookkeeping skills were limited to the ability to balance a personal checking account. As a journalism major in college I had a very well-rounded liberal arts education; however, this included only one course from the business department and that was general economics. Prior to purchasing Sandy Point Resort I could tell you all about the "consumption function," and explain the guns vs. butter model; however, I didn't know a thing about double-entry bookkeeping. I was, however, taught to be a quick study and knew how to research any topic by means of diving in and gathering as much information as possible.

Before I purchased bookkeeping software, I bought and read a book called, *If You Can Read, You Can Learn Double-Sided Accounting*. Unfortunately, this book is now out-of-print, but there are many others available to teach you the basic concept of double-entry bookkeeping. Remember, assets are things you own and liabilities are things you owe, and every item you post in your books needs to fall into one category or the other. But each credit entry must be balanced by a debit entry and this isn't always easy to figure out until you understand double-entry bookkeeping. Also there are computer programs other than AccountEdge such as QuickBooks Pro, for example, which will walk you through a step-by-step process when setting up your system. Have a reliable computer and get in the habit of backing up your data on a regular basis.

Also, do budget for a reliable, professional accountant to prepare your annual tax returns. If you provide him or her with neat, detailed bookkeeping records, you shouldn't have to pay more than $800 per year to keep the I.R.S. paid and satisfied.

Chapter 4:
The Business Plan Itself

Professionally-speaking, I am not only an innkeeper with 20 years experience in the field, I am also a journalist, editor and author. My last three books were novels and a rule I follow when writing fiction is: "show don't tell." So far in providing tips on writing a business plan, even though it's obviously not fiction, it's been nothing but tell-tell-tell.

The material that follows is where I *show* you how it's done. Please note, this should not be considered a "start-up" business plan, but rather, a plan with figures and examples of information to help you start your own plan to detemrine the feasibility of your adventure and your presentation to potential investors. Also note, it will behoove you greatly to factor out the figures over a five-year period. I suggest you aim for profit in five years.

Use the following pages as an example when writing your own business plan, and expect to find a few things that you may not have thought about. For example, it never occurred to us when we first purchased Sandy Point Resort that the area did not have 911 emergency service (or that we'd need to use it!). We now have it, as well as cell phone service, but we didn't even have service for AT&T (the world's largest carrier?) until the summer of 2011.

The more details you cover in your business plan, the better prepared you'll be to become a successful innkeeper.

Business Plan

for

Sandy Point Resort and Disc Golf Ranch

Lac du Flambeau,

Vilas County, WI

January, 2012

Prepared by

Michele V. Cozzens

Table of Contents

Concept

Description of Property

Services Provided

Physical Structures

Location

History of Business

Marketing Plan

Personnel

Consultants and Outside Resources

Expansion Opportunities

Financial Information

Concept

Sandy Point Resort and Disc Golf Ranch is a family-owned and operated vacation facility located in the Northwoods of Wisconsin and takes pride in calling itself the "World's First Disc Golf Resort." Fully furnished and equipped cabins are available for rent on a nightly or weekly basis at both on-season and off-season rates. Costs of the cabin rental include all resort accommodations, waterfront and disc golf course facilities. Additionally, the disc golf course is open to the public for a daily green fee, and hosts one to two PDGA (Professional Disc Golf Association) sanctioned tournaments each year.

Description of the Business

Sandy Point, a sole-proprietorship, is a traditional, family-owned and operated Northwoods resort. It is open seasonally from May 1 until November 1. Sandy Point resides on 45 acres of heavily wooded property with 510-feet of sandy lake frontage. It carries a "Recreational" zoning, which qualifies as commercial property. Sandy Point has been open to the public for vacation purposes since the mid-1930s. The Cozzens family has owned the property since 1992.

Seven rental units, "housekeeping cabins," are available to the public for rent at nightly and weekly rates. Rental rates cover the use of all resort facilities, including use of the 27-hole disc (Frisbee) golf course. A pro shop/gift store, featuring Innova golf discs and disc golf related products and Dream Life Designs handcrafted jewelry are on site. Owners also maintain an online retail presence.

Services Provided

Each furnished cabin is a self-contained unit with personal parking space for automobiles and trailers. Guests receive cabin key/s upon registration. Cabins are clean/sanitized upon guest arrival. They are equipped with a full kitchen (stove, oven, refrigerator, microwave oven, coffee maker, cooking and eating utensils). Outdoor Weber grill/grill tools are also provided. One set of bed linens is provided for each bed (made-up upon guest arrival) as well as extra sheets, blankets, pillows for convertible furniture. Private bathrooms are equipped with toilet tissue supply. Cabins offer flat-screen, H-D televisions, DVD/video players and boom boxes. Satellite Internet service is available on site and most cell phone providers are accessible. Each cabin has a screen porch and outdoor furniture, including a picnic table and a private fire pit. Firewood is for sale on property. Rental rates include exclusive use of a private 14-foot rowboat, a resort canoe and paddleboats. Two 90-foot docks are available for mooring personal watercraft. Rental rates also include full access to the on site fish cleaning hut, disc golf course and use of golf discs, as well as access to volleyball court, basketball court, playground, and recreation house with a pool table, ping pong table, card table and pinball machine. Cabins without private laundry facilities have access to coin-operated laundry facilities on site. Owners/caretakers are on site and maintain daily office hours for concierge services, equipment repair and assistance. Snacks, soft drinks and souvenirs are for sale in the gift shop. A golf cart is available to assist guests with physical needs. Area has 911 emergency service, and the nearest hospital, clinic and urgent care facilities are within 15 miles. Two 24-hour grocery stores are 15 minutes away. Numerous restaurants, shops and attractions, as well as campgrounds, biking trails, ATV, snowmobile trails, and hiking trails are also nearby. The 27-hole disc golf course is open to the public and a daily green fee includes the use of golf discs. (Children under age 12 are free of charge for disc golf). A public restroom is on site and green fees include use of a picnic area near the course and access to the Wisconsin Disc Golf Hall of Fame, located on property. Lakefront facilities are exclusive to resort guests renting cabins. There is no camping allowed at Sandy Point Resort.

Physical Structures
Owner's Home: Cedar-sided, asphalt shingle, full log accents. Chalet-style. 7+ bedroom, 3 bathrooms, 2 offices; 2 kitchens, dining, living areas; professional laundry facilities/utility and storage areas; cedar summer room; two outdoor decks; extensive gardens.

Main Garage: Cedar-sided, asphalt shingle, ranch-style. Two active bays for automobile storage. Includes large work and tool/equipment storage area, extensive trash/recycling storage area; retail product storage area.

Resort Office/Pro Shop: Cedar-sided, asphalt shingle, full log accents, chalet-style. Consists of four rooms and a large front porch/deck. Paved, striped public parking area.

Wash House: Half-log sided, asphalt shingle, ranch-style. Public toilet/restroom; coin-operated laundry facilities. Independent septic system.

Recreation House: Half-log sided 24 x 32, asphalt shingle, large outdoor deck. Hardwood floor. Home of the Wisconsin Disc Golf Hall of Fame.

Firewood Hut: Half-log sided, asphalt shingle, dirt floor.

Fish Cleaning Hut: RB&B sided, asphalt shingle, screened, Chalet-style.

Boat House: Plywood sided, asphalt shingle, shed-style.

Rental Cabin #1: "Karibu," built in 1936. Traditional log-style 20 x 24. Cedar logs, asphalt shingles. Two bedrooms, one bathroom with shower, kitchen/dining/living areas, screened porch. Outdoor picnic area. Annexed parking space. Seasonal, open May 1-October 1.

Rental Cabin #2: "Hilltop," built in 2001. Half-log sided, asphalt shingles. 24 x 32 modified ranch-style. Two bedrooms, one full bathroom, kitchen/dining/living areas, screen porch. Outdoor picnic area, parking. Seasonal, open May 1-October 1.

Rental Cabin #3-1/2: "The Marq," built in 1998. Modified Chalet-style. Cedar-sided, asphalt shingles. Year-round unit. Three bedrooms, two full bathrooms, kitchen, dining/living areas, river rock wood-burning fireplace, screen porch. Outdoor picnic area.

Rental Cabin #5: "The Big House," built in 2001. Chalet-style. Half-log sided, asphalt shingles. Year-round unit. Three bedrooms, two full bathrooms, kitchen, dining/living areas, river rock wood-burning fireplace, screen porch, deck. Outdoor picnic area.

Rental Cabin #6: "Stickeen," built in 1994. 24 x 36 ranch style. Half-log sided, asphalt shingles. Two bedrooms, one full bath, kitchen/dining/living areas, wood-burning fireplace, screen porch. Outdoor picnic area.

Rental Cabin #7: "Aerie," built in 1994. 24 x 36 ranch style. Half-log sided, asphalt shingles. Two bedrooms, one full bath, kitchen/dining/ living areas, wood-burning fireplace, screen porch. Outdoor picnic area.

Annexed Property Rental Unit: "Lakeview Lodge." Built 1945, purchased in 1995, updated/remodeled 1996/2011. Half-log and RB&B siding, asphalt shingle, chalet-style. Four bedrooms, three bathrooms, two kitchens/living/dining areas. Screen porch; deck, outdoor picnic area/garden.

Annexed Property Garage 1: RB&B sided, asphalt shingle, two-car garage and storage area.

Annexed Property Garage 2: Aluminum sided, aluminum roof, in-floor hydro-electric heat. Three bays, laundry and storage area.

Annexed Property Caretaker Dwelling: Aluminum sided, aluminum roof, one bedroom, one bathroom, dining/living area, kitchen, outdoor picnic area/garden.

27-Hole Disc Golf Course: Professionally-designed disc golf course located on approximately 25 acres of heavily-wooded resort property. The course consists of 27 galvanized steel/chain link basket targets and tee signs, concrete tee pads, wooden benches.

Location

Sandy Point Resort is located in north-central Wisconsin, USA, on the north shore of 785-acre Squaw Lake in Vilas County, in the township of Lac du Flambeau. Forty-five minutes from Eagle River, the county seat, and fifteen minutes from the island city of Minocqua, the nearest major metropolitan area is Minneapolis/St. Paul, which is a four-hour drive. Accessible by paved roads, two and four lane highways and Interstate routes. The nearest municipal airport is Rhinelander/Oneida County, located 45 minutes away by car.

History of Business

Sandy Point Resort, originally named Camp Fire Lodge, began as the residence of the Simon E. Anderson family in the early 1930s. In addition to the residence on property, they built five rental cabins with cedar logs harvested from the original 40-acre plot. The property also housed an ice shed and a store, and catered to guests and lake residents for basic necessities. The original cabins (only one of which still stands today) were not equipped with indoor plumbing. A public shower/bath house and individual outhouses were available for guest use. Guests also took meals prepared by Mrs. Alma Anderson at the main house. A series of owners took turns updating the cabins to provide full kitchens and bathrooms. Purchased by the Bickelhoff family in 1952, they named the property Sandy Point Resort for the sugar sand beach on the north shore of Squaw Lake. In the 1980s the original store was moved by owner Dan Doorn, and became the first "recreation house." An owner's garage/storage area was built in place of the former store. At this time, the owners' residence was also remodeled and expanded.

The current owners, the Cozzens, took over Sandy Point in 1992 and had their first summer of operation in 1993. Immediately they began work designing and building the disc golf course. Once established (the sixth disc golf course to establish in the state of Wisconsin), it went from nine to 18 to 24 to finally, 27 holes. In 1994 they built two new cabins (#6, "Stickeen" and #7 "Aerie") providing year round facilities for the first time in the resort's history. In 1998 they demolished two of the original cabins (#3, "Seldom Inn" or "Wolf Den," and #4, "Honeymoon" or "Ivan's Lure") and built one in their place, calling it cabin #3-1/2, "The Marq." In 2001, two more cabins were razed (#5, "The Big House" or "Uncommon Loon," and #2, "Hilltop," or "Zeke's Lair,"). The cabins replacing them were dubbed with the original names, "The Big House" and "Hilltop." The old store/ recreation house was also razed in 2001 and replaced with a new building. In 1999, they constructed a new front office and pro shop, and added the public restroom and laundry/wash house in 2008.

After operating Sandy Point Resort as a year-round facility until 2001, the Cozzens decided to return to a seasonal format. The resort is currently open to the public from May 1 until November 1. The disc golf baskets, however, remain in the ground year-round and the course is open to the pubic, weather (snow) permitting.

Marketing

Tourism is big business in the state of Wisconsin and the Northwoods is one of the state's most attractive and lucrative vacation destinations. According to the Wisconsin Department of Tourism, in 2010 "pleasure travel" accounted for 71 percent of $12.3 billon in Wisconsin travelers' dollars. Lodging accounted for 13 percent and recreation accounted for 22 percent of dollars spent. $255 million was spent in Vilas County, ranking it tenth in the state, and $202 million was spent in neighboring Oneida County, ranking it seventeenth. According to a survey conducted by national research firm, Davidson-Peterson Associates, traveler spending in Wisconsin during 2010 increased 1.8 percent over 2009.

Sandy Point customers, Wisconsin travelers, renting cabins are predominantly young families, with children ranging in age from 1-18. A majority of travelers originate from Wisconsin, Minnesota, Illinois, Iowa, Michigan, Indiana and Missouri. They come from any number of places, including California, Arizona, Colorado, New York and Georgia, for example, but all tend to have ties to the state of Wisconsin. Sandy Point is an excellent location for family reunions, often catering to multiple generations. Guests appreciate the spacious, clean and well-maintained cabins and grounds, and are responsible for a great deal of word-of-mouth advertising.

Off-season rates are available during the months of May, September and October. Weekly rates are available during the summer months, which discount the on-season nightly rates. For example, one two-bedroom unit has an on-season rate of $205 per night. The on-season weekly rate is $975. This represents a 32 percent discount.

Sandy Point capitalizes on its distinction as being the "world's first disc golf resort." Disc golf enthusiasts, both professional and recreational players, seek accommodations, primarily in the shoulder or off-season periods. Each year Sandy Point hosts one-to-two bachelor parties because of its disc golf course. (These same groups often return with wives and girlfriends for honeymoons and anniversaries). The disc golf course attracts local players as well as golfers traveling from long distances and foreign countries. Local camps, churches and recreational groups regularly schedule outings and even tournaments on property.

Sandy Point Resort is one of three resorts located on Squaw Lake. On the lake, it is by far the largest in terms of property, lake frontage and accommodations. According to the properties registered with the Minocqua Area Chamber of Commerce and/or the Minocqua Area

Resorts Association, there are approximately 50 family-owned and operated resorts within a 15-20 mile radius.

In addition to a large percentage of word-of-mouth referrals for cabin rentals, Sandy Point Resort attracts customers primarily through the World Wide Web. A detailed, complex website (www.sandypt. com) includes resort, cabin, personnel information, rates, availability, photos, testimonials, a blog and a contact form. A toll-free number, 888-588-3233, is offered to potential guests for making inquiries and reservations.

Sandy Point is a member of the Lac du Flambeau Chamber of Commerce and the Minocqua Area Resorts Association (MARA), which includes listings on their websites and a referral network. Sandy Point is also listed on a number of vacation property websites. It has a business Facebook page, currently networking with over 1,100 users.

The World Wide Web accounts for most new business for cabin rentals; however, newspaper ads in the local community newspaper, *The Lakeland Times*, are placed regularly, specifically advertising the disc golf course and pro shop, and Dream Life Designs jewelry. Membership in the Professional Disc Golf Association (PDGA), as well as PDGA-sanctioned tournaments afford listings and marketing to the worldwide disc golf community. The disc golf course is listed on several course directories and review sites.

Personnel

Michael B. Cozzens. Property owner since 1992. Disc Golf enthusiast since 1974. Member of the PDGA (#3168); tournament director; course designer; Innova golf disc specialist; noted glo-disc collector. Keen knowledge of electrical and plumbing systems, construction, small equipment and automotive repair and maintenance. Construction project/s designer and supervisor; Maintenance staff supervisor; Works on cleaning crew; Pro shop sales; Internet sales; Telephone sales.

Michele V. Cozzens. Property owner since 1992. Member of the PDGA (#4171); Operations supervisor; Bookkeeping; Marketing, Advertising, Graphic Design and Internet site maintenance; Manages cleaning staff and housekeeping supplies; Decorating; Budgeting; Guest services; Pro shop sales; Internet sales; Telephone sales; Chief buyer and designer for Dream Life Designs jewelry and pro shop/gift shop.

Willow G. Cozzens. Born in 1995. PDGA #9873. Cleaning staff; guest services; pro shop sales; babysitting.

Camille E. Cozzens. Born in 1997. PDGA #13001. Cleaning staff; guest services; pro shop sales; babysitting.

Scott "Stu" Cook. Year-round resident caretaker and full time grounds maintenance; disc golf course landscaping; disc golfer; pro shop sales; area naturalist; guest services; cleaning, odd jobs, and maintenance crews. PDGA #16503

Consultants and Outside Resources
Accountant: Angelo DiFonzo
Associations: Lac du Flambeau Chamber of Commerce; Minocqua-Area-Resort Association; Professional Disc Golf Association
Attorney: Timothy Melms
Carpenter: Bryan Nelson
Electrical Company: Price Electric
Exterminator: Diamondback Pest Management
Insurance Agency: Insurance Center, Rhinelander
Plumber: Van Natta Plumbing
Propane Supplier: Ritchie Oil and Propane
Septic Specialist: Mike Pleasant
Webmaster: Shawn Sinclair
Well and Pump Specialist: Hanser Well and Pump

Expansion Opportunities
    Prior to the Cozzens' takeover in 1992, income from cabin rentals accounted for 98 percent of the resort income. (Two percent came from motor rentals and incidentals). Building the disc golf course

and retail operation along with new, larger and more modern rental cabins with year round rental potential, have been successful expansion projects generating more annual income. Today income percentages are as follows: cabin rentals 55 percent; disc golf green fees: 5 percent; golf disc sales: 30 percent; jewelry sales: 5 percent; motor rentals/additional retail: 5 percent. Overall income has expanded ten times over.

One income-generating project under consideration is to expand the resort office/pro shop building to include a clubhouse with eating area and coffee shop, which is open to resort guests and the public. Additionally, the resort plans to also once again offer year-round facilities and market to snowmobilers and cross-country skiers. Finally, the resort plans to host not one, but two PDGA-sanctioned disc golf tournaments beginning in 2012.

Financial Information*
Income:

The following projected annual income is based on renting seven cabins at on-season, 2012 rates, 100% occupancy for a total of 12 weeks.

Cabin #1, "Karibu:" $725/wk. x 12 weeks = $8,700
Cabin #2, "Hilltop:" $925/wk. x 12 weeks = $11,100
Cabin #3-1/2, "The Marq:" $1,700 wk. x 12 weeks = $20,400
Cabin #5, "The Big House:" $1,800 wk. x 12 weeks = $21,600
Cabin #6, "Stickeen;" $975/wk. x 12 weeks = $11,700
Cabin #7, "Aerie:" $975/wk. x 12 weeks = $11,700
Cabin #8, "Lakeview Lodge:" $2,400/wk. x 12 weeks = $28,800.
Total cabin income = $114,000.00

Expenses:

Accounting fees: $775
Advertising: $2,200
Autos/Gas-powered engines: $2,900
Credit Card Fees: $1,600
Decorating: $525
Dues/Memberships: $185
Guest Amenities: $1,225

Housekeeping Supplies: $2,800
Insurance: (buildings, autos, liability, personal health) $7,600
Maintenance and Repair: $15,000
Office Expenses: $6,700
Seasonal Help: $11,500
Security Monitoring: $200
Taxes/Licenses: $18,000
Utilities: (electric, propane, septic, telephone, trash) $14,200

Total Operating Expenses: $85,410

Estimated Net Profit: $28,590

Financial Information based on the very important concept of estimating income low and expenses high. Income estimate takes into account cabin rentals only. Expenses based on real operating costs from calendar year 2011.

Chapter 5:
Policies and Procedures

You may or may not want to include your policies and procedures in your business plan, but either way, it's important to understand that developing workable operating systems in advance will be a key to your success. A good business manager will develop a written account of all the property's policies and procedures. You don't need to write a book; however, having a readable, accessible explanation of how the business operates is a valuable tool for many reasons, particularly if you need someone else to run your business due to unforeseen circumstances. It's also good for potential employees and for prospective buyers if and when you choose to sell your business.

A good business manager will also understand the need to be both rigid and flexible where these policies and procedures are concerned. What do I mean?

I assure you that while our reservations, maintenance and turnover procedures haven't changed much since the beginning of our tenure as innkeepers, our policies have definitely evolved. As we learned on the job over many years, some issues or techniques needed tweaking. I must remind you again that innkeepers need to be flexible. Further, you must be willing to ask for advice about what works for your colleagues, and you must understand when a policy needs to be amended.

Pet Policy

One policy we have changed several times is our pet policy. We started out allowing dogs on property. We have never allowed cats (due to our own cat allergies and because allergies to cats are widespread among the general public, i.e. our guests). And after the first time a guest brought a large, white squawking cockatoo without warning, we specifically excluded "birds and other exotics." We limited the number of guest dogs on property to two, and guests electing to bring dogs were charged a refundable fifty-dollar cleaning/damage deposit. Dog owners are further required to register their dogs when they make their reservations, and agree to not leave dogs unattended in cabins or tied to trees. Most importantly, they agree to leave no evidence of their dogs behind (indoors or outdoors).

After ten years and countless violations to our policy, we gave up. We no longer allowed dogs during the on-season, summer months. We hated doing this to our regular customers who brought well-behaved dogs and always cleaned up after them; however, in spite of the refundable cleaning and damage deposits, not every dog owner cared about getting back the fifty-dollar deposit. And on the one day of the week (Saturday) when we have a mere six hours to turnover seven cabins and the grounds, we simply didn't have the time or the staff to repair pawed-out screens, or pick out individual dog hairs from chenille throw pillows, or wash every blanket, quilt, pillow sham and bed skirt covered with Fido's fur.

Another problem was with the refundable cleaning/damage deposit. In the rare event that we found it necessary to keep the deposit, nearly every dog-owner objected. The policy violators felt violated themselves, and called us everything from "greedy" to "delusional." In 2003 one violator, according to our caretaker at the time, brought a dog without preregistering and soiled not one but three cabins during the stay of his large, family group. After I wrote a brief note informing him we'd be keeping his deposit, we received a letter so scathing and mean-spirited, that we couldn't help but laugh. Especially when we noticed in the lower left corner that it was dictated to and typed by his secretary. It read: *"You, in the words of Shakespeare 'protesteth too much' ... way too much. Your letter is marginally anal. Maybe it just happens if one throws too many Frisbees. ... I hope you really need the $50 you snarfed more than me, and that you dutifully report its receipt to the IRS. I'm telling all my friends to visit your resort ... you'll be booked solid this summer."*

In another case a dog owner actually swore her pet had not left scratches, nor was there a carpet full of dog hairs for us to clean. When we kept her deposit, she too threatened that she'd never come back nor would any of her family or friends.

We are not delusional when it comes to spotting recent damage or identifying dog hairs. We know what dog hairs look like, and we understand why they're there when we do find them. Very simply, it's because a dog was in the unit and the owner did not clean up. In one unit, where a dog hasn't been since the 2009 off-season, I occasionally STILL find a basset hound hair or two in the cracks of the screened porch.

We have always allowed dogs to come in the off-season. And last summer, due to the economy causing lower occupancy levels than normal, as well as an inordinate number of cancellations, we found it necessary to relax our strict policy during the on-season. We allowed guests to bring their dogs on a pre-approved basis, with the goal of filling those vacancies. We therefore amended the policy once again, and followed guidelines set up by several hotels in which we have stayed with our dog. In addition to the cleaning and damage deposit, we charged a fee. Our hope is that by increasing the value of the amenity, those who opt to take advantage of it will be more appreciative and respectful of the policy. We chalk it up to accepting the pet issue as one of the ills from an innkeeper's Pandora's Box, and understand that in the same way people will be people, dogs will be dogs and some people will believe their dogs are people too.

I guarantee you that every dog owner who asks to bring a dog will tell you at least one of the following things: "Our dog is like our child;" "We never go anywhere without our dog;" "Our dog went to obedience school and is very well behaved;" "Our dog always stays in a crate and is trained to stay off the furniture;" "Our dog never barks;" "Our dog is very small and you won't even know she's around." Dog owners wholeheartedly believe each of these statements about their dogs to be 100 percent true.

Let me make it very clear that in some cases these proclamations are indeed, 100 percent true, and not all dog owners have been guilty of not cleaning up after their dogs. In fact, a majority of guest dogs were very well behaved and there was no sign of them being in the cabins or on the grounds upon guests' departures. But all it takes is one barking, howling dog at five in the morning, who is upset about his owner leaving him behind while he goes fishing, and you've just ruined a vacation day for any guests in surrounding cabins who had hoped to spend the morning sleeping in!

By the way, we have a dog. She's a six-pound chihuahua named Cinco, and if you stay at Sandy Point during the summer, chances are you will see Cinco *and* you will hear her. She tends to yap at other dogs and strangers—particularly men—and for some reason our caretaker Stu, even though she's known him for seven years. Her yappy bark annoys the stink out of me and *I* actually love this little dog. So I can only imagine what *you* must think of her! Nevertheless, we are highly conscious of her yappiness and try to keep it at a minimum to not annoy the otherwise peaceful atmosphere of the resort. And by the way, we transport Cinco back-and-forth to Sandy Point Resort by plane, and the airlines charge $100 to $150 each way just to keep her in a soft crate under the seat in front of us. So, believe-you-me, if your dog is like your kid, it's going to cost ya!

The following is our pet agreement, found on our website and presented to dog-owning guests for signature.

PET AGREEMENT

Sandy Point Resort and Disc Golf Ranch allows dogs in resort cabins per designation and personal arrangement with the management. The charge is $15/day or $60/week. We do not allow cats, birds or other exotics. Please do not ask us to make exceptions. DOGS ARE NOT ALLOWED ON PROPERTY DURING THE NORTHWOODS OPEN TOURNAMENT, held each Labor Day weekend. The size, number and breed of dogs may be restricted at the discretion of management. If you would like to bring your dog, it must arranged IN ADVANCE of your arrival, and in conjunction with your reservation. All dog reservations must be confirmed in writing. A refundable $50 cleaning/damage deposit, payable by separate check only at reservation is also required. Guests who bring dogs without written advanced confirmation will be fined $100. If a dog is discovered on property during guest stay, guests will be asked to leave at once and cabin rentals fees will not be refunded. With this invitation, we expect you to respect the following considerations for the property and our other guests. Failure to comply will result in the loss of your deposit. The decision to keep a cleaning/damage deposit is solely at the discretion of the property owners/caretakers as advised by the housekeeping staff.

DOGS ARE NOT ALLOWED AT THE BEACH WHEN OTHER GUESTS ARE PRESENT.

X _____ Dogs must be managed at all times. Dog owners are responsible for cleaning up after their dogs in their cabin and the common areas of the resort. At NO TIME is the dog allowed outside of the cabin without being accompanied by the owner and dog MUST be on a leash.

X _____ You are not to leave your dog in your cabin unattended while you are not on resort property. If you need to leave the resort for any reason, you are to take your dog with you. Failure to do so could result in a breach of this agreement.

X _____ If we receive any noise complaints about your dog, you will receive notice advising you to keep your dog under control. If we receive a second complaint, you will be asked to remove your dog from the resort property.

X _____ Dogs are not allowed on the furniture and particularly the beds. We prefer dogs to be kenneled at night. If your dog regularly sleeps with you, Sandy Point is not the place for you to bring him/her. Any evidence of dog hair on furniture or bedding will result in forfeiture of deposit.

Please treat your cabin, other guests and the resort property with the same care as you would your permanent home. Any damage to the cabin or property—or evidence of your dog (i.e. pet waste/shedding/scratch marks) will result in loss of cleaning/damage deposit.

Please provide the following information about your pet:

Dog's name: _____   Breed: _____

Weight: _____   Age: _____   Dog Deposit check #: _____

ACKNOWLEDGEMENT AND AGREEMENT OF THE ABOVE PET POLICY:

_____   _____
PRINT NAME   CELL/CONTACT NUMBER

_____   _____
SIGNATURE   DATE

Keep this in mind when establishing your pet policy: It's one thing to tolerate sharing your property with humans who are strangers, and yet quite another to share it with strange animals. Obviously it's important to not only establish your pet policy, but also to be prepared to enforce it. It will—repeat WILL—account for occasional awkward or uncomfortable moments. Over time, however, you will get better at handling most of these moments.

By the way, if anyone ever shows up on your property with a blue-eyed crow in a cage (in spite of your policy of "no birds or other exotics"), beware. Truly, the pet crow named George was the most bizarre violation we've had of our pet policy in two decades of operation. Our daughter, Willow, was leery about this crow's presence on property during the summer of 2011. She called it a "soul stealer." Well, I believe my soul remained in tact, however, George certainly stole my will to tell his owner that birds weren't allowed. Frankly, since I'd never met a pet crow, I was fascinated. George turned out to be a delightful guest for the week except for one thing. When he and his owners left, we discovered a screen porch screen splattered with crow shit, which we (or I should say my husband) had to clean.

Reservations and Cancellations

Approximately 75 percent of our summer guests are repeat customers who make their reservations a year in advance. We give regular guests "first refusal" on the cabins in which they stayed for the same week the following summer. I therefore have a calendar for 2013 ready during the summer of 2012, and know the exact dates that correspond to the guests' intended future stay. Each year they change a little bit. Most years it's just a day. When leap years figure into the mix, it's a two-day change. And then every six years, our calendar requires an adjustment that inevitably leaves some guests baffled and under the impression that we're trying to shift or change their regular week. We're not. On the contrary, we're making provisions to keep their weeks the same.

We call it the year of the "big jump." The last one was in 2009 and the next one will be in 2015. To figure out weekly dates, as a rule we use holidays like Memorial Day, Father's Day, the 4th of July and Labor Day. Memorial Day is always the last Monday in May, Father's Day the second Sunday in June, the 4th of July is, of course, a given, and Labor Day is the first Monday in September. Using our 4th of July guests, The Hoffman family, who originally hail from Menasha, WI as examples, they've gathered together at Sandy Point from places as far as California and Colorado every summer for nearly as long as we've owned the resort. The first time the Hoffmans came, all of the original cabins were still standing and it was before our daughters were born. We love having them stay and as we all grow old and older together each summer, we refer to them as "our 4th of July family." As they reserve five of our seven cabins for the 4th of July week, we must check the calendar to be sure the Hoffman butts are in our beds on the night of the 4th. Since we rent from Saturday to Saturday, when the 4th falls on a Saturday, it may be when we have to make the big jump, and their dates will change from June 28 - July 5, 2014 to July 4 – 11, 2015. It may seem like they're coming a week later, however, it's still the "4th of July week." The weeks surrounding the 4th adjust accordingly.

Guests making reservations for the first time more often than not make them by calling our toll free phone line. I highly recommend offering a toll free reservation and information line. When potential guests search the web for accommodations, chances are they have a list of many places to call. Who will they call first? The place that doesn't cost them long-distance phone charges. Be forewarned, however, that toll free numbers also attract callers who don't really intend to book a room or cabin with you, but instead use you as an area information line. It's easy to decipher a caller's true intentions shortly into the conversation, and when I'm hit with a whole lot of area information questions rather than questions specific to our resort or disc golf course, I graciously direct the caller to the toll free line of the local Chamber of Commerce.

Our website has an availability calendar on it for each day and week of the year and each cabin. It's important to always keep this calendar current. The minute I take a reservation I block out the dates to read, "BOOKED," and on the flip side, delete the booking in case of a cancellation. To web browsers, all cabins available for reservation read: "AVAILABLE" under the corresponding dates. In our website administrator, viewable only to us, I record the details including name, address, number of days, number of people, amount of deposit received and method of payment (check or credit card) and any notes specific to the guest or reservation, such as whether or not the guest is a returning customer or if they'll be celebrating a birthday or anniversary. We also maintain a paper calendar called "the reservation book." It tends to be more portable and convenient than any of our computers. I constantly cross-reference the two reservation records and pay very close attention so that I don't make the capital error of double-booking.

It took 19 years for me to make a double-booking mistake. I'm not sure how it happened other than to chalk it up to either oversight or mommy-brain, but it proved to me that what I thought was a fool proof system still required that I not make a foolish mistake. Fortunately at the time of the incident we had another, larger two-bedroom unit available, and I was able to offer one of the double-book-ees a "free upgrade," which he gladly accepted. Whew!

Whether or not guests are first-timers or have been returning for years, we require a deposit to confirm their reservations. Deposits of $150 or $250 (10-20 percent of cabin rental costs) are non-refundable. Guests who cancel reservations have the opportunity to reapply deposits within the same calendar year, but only if we're able to rebook their cabin. Guests who cancel reservations within two weeks of expected arrival forfeit their deposits, regardless of whether or not we are able to rebook the cabin. You'll need to do a lot of scrambling to fill last-minute cancellations. This is where membership in local associations and other forms of social networking like Facebook, for example, show their true values.

In some cases, regular guests may need to cancel but don't want to permanently lose their regular week/cabin. If they ask to simply skip a year and you're willing to make this concession for them, be sure to tell the guests who fill the cancellation that they may not have first refusal for the following year.

As I like to keep all income on a calendar year fiscal program, we do not take summer deposits a year in advance. Instead, we send notices during the first week of December and ask for deposits by a January 20 deadline. This system serves two purposes. One, it gives guests an out if they need it—especially because a lot of unforeseeable circumstances may arise in a year. For example, over the holidays potential guests may find out that a cousin or sister is getting married during their usual vacation week. Or maybe their employers don't allow vacation scheduling until the first of the year. Maybe, heaven forbid, they've developed an illness or have lost a job. I can't tell you how many guests we've lost during the past three years due to job loss.

This is the third economic downturn we've experienced while in the innkeeping business. During the brief recessions of the early 1990s and early 2000s, we didn't notice a drop off in business. Our observation was that vacationers may have been giving up on the bigger trips to places like Europe, Hawaii and Disneyland, but they could still afford to load up the car and drive to the Northwoods. With consistent, 100 percent seasonal occupancy, we may have been fooled into believing our innkeeping operation was recession-proof. This latest economic downturn, however, has made a stronger impression and we, like every small business, have had to do a lot of adjusting and belt-tightening, and at the same time, be sensitive to the living conditions and financial situations of our guests.

The second reason for collecting deposits in January is because annual first half property taxes in Wisconsin are due January 31. Since the resort closes in November and the bulk of our income essentially comes to halt, we count on the summer deposits to pay that sizeable bill. By the way, the subject of property taxes is confusing. I can't help but wonder why our property values have dropped significantly in market value; however, our property taxes have not dropped proportionately—or at all. Nevertheless, it's a very important bill and it accounts for nearly 10 percent of our business overhead expense.

Once we receive deposits we confirm reservations via email. For those guests who don't have email, we simply mail a paper copy to their home address. The following is a copy of our reservation confirmation, which includes a list of guidelines to reiterate answers to questions we have already most likely answered during the reservation process. I can't stress enough the importance of communicating your policies and provisions as many times as possible, particularly to new guests.

The balance of rental fees is due at registration and the original deposit is deducted from the amount due. This includes cabin rental fees, motor rental if applicable, extra occupant fees as well as state and local taxes. Since we don't have incidental charges like in-room telephones or pay-per-view television, for example, unlike a hotel we don't require a credit card number to remain on file. I recommend collecting all fees up front so you don't run the risk of dealing with guests who might leave the property without paying—either accidentally or on purpose. Plus, in the event that you receive a bad check

Guest Name
Guest Address
Guest Phone

Arrival Date/Time:
Departure Date:
Cabin Rented:
Number in Party: (Adults, children, babies under 1 year)
Rental Rate: + 8.5% tax
Special Requests:
Deposit Received:

Downloadable Map of the Resort:
http://www.sandypt.com/The-Resort/Resort-Map.html

SANDY POINT GUIDELINES FOR CABIN RENTERS

Hello and **Thank You** for booking a cabin with us! This is your reservation confirmation. The following list of guidelines is provided to
help you with your pre-arrival questions. If you have any questions
after reading this information, please feel free to write: michele@
sandypt.com or call our toll-free phone line: 888-588-3233.

1. Check in time is 4 p.m. Sorry, but we cannot accommodate early
check-ins during the summer season. If you plan to arrive after 7
p.m., we may not be available to register you until the following
morning. A note will be left on the front door of the office and your
cabin lights will be on. If you're new to Sandy Point, instructions on
how to get to your cabin will be provided. We ask that you come to
the office at 10 a.m. the next morning to register and pay the balance of fees.

2. With the exception of late arrivals, cabins will be locked until you
pay the balance of your fees and obtain a key from the front office.

Payment may be made by cash, personal check, VISA, Mastercard or Discover cards.

3. Please inform us of any additional guests who plan to arrive during your stay. As our facilities are for registered guests only, we require that all visitors check-in at the office. Overnight guests – beyond your cabin's base-rate occupancy level of 4, 6, or 8 – cost an additional $20 each per night or $60 per week, and daily visitors/ non-resort guests planning to spend time and use resort facilities beyond a brief visit ($20 per vehicle) must pay fees in advance. All autos must be registered. No camping or tents allowed.

4. We do not supply food, towels, paper or cleaning products of any kind. For the sake of our septic systems, the toilet tissue supply should be adequate; however, if you need more you must supply it. Additional trash bags are also your responsibility.

5. Mandatory trash recycling is the law in Wisconsin. Our trash policy is posted inside each cabin.

6. To maintain cleanliness and as a courtesy to the guests who follow you, we ask that you please smoke outside or use the screened porch for smoking. Also, please dispose of your cigarette butts properly – in waste cans as opposed to on the grounds.

7. We expect you to leave your cabin clean and report all damage or breakage. As we're trying to avoid charging cleaning/damage deposits, we provide a list of housekeeping guidelines inside each cabin and thank you for your cooperation. Please note that we do not offer laundry or sheet exchange services. There is a public laundry facility on property. Check-out times are 9 a.m. (on season) and 11 a.m. (off season or by permission according to reservation).

CANCELLATIONS
All deposits received are considered non-refundable. If you must cancel your reservations, you may reapply deposits prior to arrival to other weeks within the same calendar year, only where vacancies exist, and only if we are able to rebook your cabin. Any cancel-

lation made (for whatever reason) less than two weeks prior to your scheduled arrival, will resort in the forfeiture of your deposit.

You will get one opportunity to reapply your deposit. If a second cancellation occurs on the same deposit, you will forfeit the deposit. Off-season guests, or those who book cabins for less than a week, who must cut short nightly reservations face a $50 cancellation fee. No-shows will surrender any deposits received and face an additional $50 no-show/cancellation fee.

We do not refund rental fees due to weather conditions or other elements indigenous to the Northwoods. If something malfunctions in your cabin, we ask that you give us the opportunity to repair or rectify the situation as soon as reasonably possible. Fees will not be refunded if you simply do not "like" your cabin, or if you exhibit unreasonable expectations.

THANK YOU FOR READING THESE GUIDELINES AND POLICIES.

Mike and Michele Cozzens
Sandy Point Resort
888-588-3233

from guests who are staying for a week, you will have time to request another form of payment prior to their departure. This has happened. In order to force guests to fill out the registration form and account for everyone and every car in their party and, of course, pay the balance of fees due when they arrive, we lock the cabins upon completing the turnover. Guests receive keys once the cabin is paid for in full.

By the way, guests will often request more than one key to their cabin, so have more than one spare available when someone inevitably gets locked out. (We have a master set as well). We do not charge for lost keys but it's something to consider as making new keys is a regular expense. Also, guests sometimes forget to leave behind keys when they vacate the property and we always call to ask them to send via mail at their earliest convenience.

Occupancy Levels and Additional Guests

It is absolutely critical that you establish occupancy limits for your rooms or units. This is based on the simple truth that the number of people you have in one space determines the amount of wear-and-tear on the unit as well as potential damages, which may cause cleaning and repair expenses to increase. Further, the more people you have on property, the more impact they have on the overall liability of your operation.

Our occupancy level policy is one on which I won't waiver. In my early years as an innkeeper I sometimes made exceptions and allowed more guests to occupy cabins than our established maximum occupancy levels; however, each and every instance was a mistake.

If you have too many people using one bathroom on a septic system, for example, I assure you the toilet will, at some point, overflow. And believe me, not one person in the oversized group will take the time to locate the cabin's plunger—even if it's in plain sight— before coming to you and asking for help.

Understand that just because a two-bedroom/one bathroom unit has two double beds, a set of bunks and a convertible sofa, and can technically sleep eight—ten if you put two more in sleeping bags on the floor—under no circumstances should you allow ten people to stay there at one time. Never. Not even if they pay extra. "We're a close-knit group," they may say. "We don't mind all staying in one cabin." My standard response to this oft-heard proposition of putting a group of ten into one two-bedroom cabin instead of two is: "You may not mind, but *I* mind, and my septic system minds as well."

FYI, in guest-speak language, "we don't mind all staying in one cabin," translates into, "we don't want to pay for more than one cabin." Our experience with guests who speak this particular language and end up coming to the resort after all, is that more often than not, we need to file them in the "high maintenance" department. It starts with a challenge to your policies and inevitably goes downhill from there.

We have established what we call "base-level" occupancy rates and "maximum-level" occupancy rates. Base-level rates are standard for the two bedroom, three bedroom and four bedroom units. The rate for any two-bedroom unit, for instance, is based on four persons or less. The cabin costs the same per night regardless if you have one, two, three or four persons staying. The maximum number of occupants in our smallest two-bedroom unit (cabin #1, "Karibu," the only remaining original cabin) is six. For the two-bedroom cabins #6, "Stickeen" and #7 "Aerie," which are larger than #1, "Karibu," the maximum occupancy rate is seven. If there are more than four guests in any of the two bedroom cabins, there is an additional charge for the extra guests of $20 per night or $60 per week. The base-rate for our three-bedroom units is six, maximum nine, and our four-bedroom unit is based upon eight, maximum 12.

Be prepared for guests (or potential guests) to ask for a discount if they have fewer occupants than your established base level. Don't do it. It's important to set up a minimum charge for the cabin, which you can expect to receive (no matter who or how many plan to stay) and budget accordingly. You may want to explain that the base rate *is* essentially a discounted rate, and that you charge more for additional guests.

And when they complain about having to pay more for their additional guests? Explain that the extra charges are meant to cover the added expenses and liabilities of having additional people on property. If you really need to break it down for yourself or your challenging guests, understand this: It's about the business overhead cost of utilities and *your* time. One additional person may take seven additional showers in a week, flush the toilet 35 more times, ring your doorbell at least five more times with a question or need for assistance, eat from another set of dishes, add to the trash levels, and increase the possibility of having some kind of accident for which he may try to blame you, sue you or pay his emergency room expenses. If the extra person is a baby in diapers, expect the trash levels to double. By the way, we don't charge for babies under the age of one. Repeat: **UNDER** the age of one. A kid that toddles up to you and calls you by name is most likely at least a year old. He or she may have been ten months old when his mommy made the reservation a year in advance, however, if and when you offer discounts for children and you mean to imply that the age of the child is relevant to the time they will be on property, be sure to state your age policy very clearly.

Most people understand the concepts of occupancy levels and limitations, but again, you must clearly communicate them during the reservation process, on your website or brochure, and reiterate them once again at check-in. Another item to address is in regard to visitors, or guests of guests. Make your visitor policy known at the time you take the reservation. Note our policy on visitors is clearly stated in item #3 of our reservation confirmation:

> "3. Please inform us of any additional guests who plan to arrive during your stay. As our facilities are for registered guests only, we require that all visitors check-in at the office. Overnight guests – beyond your cabin's base-rate occupancy level of 4, 6, or 8 – cost an additional $20 each per night or $60 per week, and daily visitors/non-resort guests planning to spend time and use resort facilities beyond a brief visit ($20 per vehicle) must pay fees in advance. All autos must be registered. No camping or tents allowed."

If you claim that the property's facilities are exclusive—paying guests only—you must establish and enforce a visitor's policy. Without a policy in place, you risk having an overcrowded facility. You certainly don't want to convey that you won't allow your guests to have visitors, and there's nothing wrong with visitors stopping by and touring the grounds. It will inevitably lead to future business. But you do want to convey that you won't allow your guests to have big, prolonged parties. Even one additional vanload of people who intend to spend the day with your paying guests will have a potentially large impact on the atmosphere of the resort and the wear-and-tear on the facilities. Remember, they're using your kitchens and bathrooms, docks, swim rafts, playgrounds and other recreational facilities. These things comprise the core of your product, and your business requires you to maintain them. To be successful, you are therefore required to charge for the use of these products. Our nominal charge for visitors is $20 per car. It's a bargain.

During the summer, particularly if it's an unusually hot summer such as the summer of 2011, it is not unusual for us to receive phone calls from neighbors or area visitors asking if we have a daily use fee for our beach. It might be a good idea to file beach use fees in the income expansion opportunity folder; however, our choice has been to keep our beach exclusive for resort guests. But not everyone phones ahead. Sometimes people just show up in their swimsuits. We are often on the lookout for those who mistake our expansive sandy beach as public property. We've found them lounging in our Adirondack chairs and having a grand time jumping on our water trampoline. One young girl, who was part of a group of eight trespassers whom I had to chase out one day, stepped on a snail on her way out of the lake and cut her foot. Five minutes later she was in my office where I tended to her cut with first aid cream and a Band-Aid. Thankfully, it wasn't a serious injury, but while I had her blood on my hands I wondered what my actual liability was for someone who walked right by the "Beach Area for Resort Guests Only" sign and jumped in the lake.

Note: We are not a public property. We are a private property that is open to the public as a commercial operation. The public to whom we are open pays to use the facilities. It doesn't make us a bad or unfriendly neighbor to deny someone the use of our property. It simply makes us savvy and seasoned business owners/operators.

Check-in and Check-out

Have you ever arrived at a hotel property earlier than you expected? Say you over-estimated your travel time or you were lucky enough to get an early start. When you ask the front desk clerk if the room you've reserved at the 200-room property is, by any chance, available for early check-in, the answer you often hear is "yes." Why? Because it's highly unlikely that the hotel was at 100 percent occupancy the night before, and their adequate cleaning/housekeeping staff has had your particular room ready for days.

There's a big difference between multi-room hotel properties and a bed-and-breakfast, small inn or family-owned and operated resort. First of all, at a resort like Sandy Point, chances of the small house-

Postcard photo of Simon and Alma Anderson, original property owners who build the resort, circa 1935. They're pictured in front of the main house, part of which still stands today.

Message on the back of postcard pictured above, September 12, 1935.

Center label reads: "Simon E. Anderson, CAMP FIRE LODGE, Squaw Lake, Lac du Flambeau, Wis." Note: the main house, pictured upper right, was painted yellow.

Circa 1937.

Walleye catch, Aug., 1950.

Mike's first fish, May, 1993.

Michele's musky, July, 2011.

Original cabins in snow, 1952.

Cabins in snow, 2012.

Owner's Home, 1993

Owner's Home, winter 2012.

Cabin #1, "Uneeda Rest," circa 1956.

Cabin #1, "Karibu," 1993. The cabin was lifted approximately three feet, and is the only remaining original cabin on property today.

Cabin #2, "Hilltop," circa 1956.

Cabin #2, "Zeke's Lair," 1993, lifted three-feet. Torn down in 2000.

The new Cabin #2, "Hilltop," built in 2001.

Cabin #4, "Honeymoon," circa 1956. Torn down in 1997.

Original store, circa 1956.

The Sandy Point Pro Shop/Office today.

Cabin #5, "The Big House," circa 1956. Torn down in 2000.

New Cabin #5, "The Big House," under construction in 2001.

View from the pier, circa 1956.

View from the pier, June, 2011.

Birch Park, circa 1956.

Birch Park Basketball Court, June, 2011.

Mike and Michele, Dakotah and Luna, winter 1993.

Joe Weinshel, Steady Ed Headrick, inventor of the modern day Frisbee, (holding Willow), Michele and Mike, May, 1995.

Willow's first winter, January, 1996.

Winter, 1996. Snow golf anyone?

"The Perfect Storm," August, 2000. Willow and Camille with an uprooted birch tree.

Microburst of July, 2008. Fourteen trees were uprooted at the lakefront including these two white pines that had once flanked the fish-cleaning hut.

Microburst of July, 2008. A poplar tree snaps in two and lands on Cabin #1, "Karibu."

Willow and Camille with Resort guest, Lily Nichols, modeling "Get Your Loon On" T-shirts, 2008.

The old, bullet-ridden car we discovered on what is now disc golf hole #22.

Willow and Camille with friends on the RAVE trampoline, June, 2006.

Wednesday evening lemonade stand with Willow and Camille (and Cinco), 2008.

Northwoods Open Tournament Director, Mike, with 3x USDGC Champion, 2x World Champion, Barry Schultz, September, 1996.

Annual Northwoods Open "Off-the-raft-hole-in-one-contest," mid-1990s.

The Cozzens Family on Squaw Lake, aboard the "Dream Life," 2003.

The Cozzens Cleaning Crew, any given summer Saturday, 2010.

The Cozzens Family, December, 2011, outside of Little Bohemia Lodge in Manitowish Waters, Wisconsin. Setting of the 1934 shootout with John Dillinger and the 2007 film *Public Enemies* starring Johnny Depp.

Michele working the desk and autographing books, 2003.

Sandy Point's front porch vintage Coke machine.

Mike's first hot stamp, "Berkeley Aquatic Park," and one of Sandy Point's custom hot stamps. Sandy Point was the sixth disc golf course to establish in the state of Wisconsin.

Hole #26. Photo credit: Terry Miller, PDGA Wisconsin State Coordinator.

keeping staff facing a 100 percent turnover prior to new guest arrival are far greater than those at the nearest Holiday Inn. Secondly, the chances of the front desk clerk also being on the cleaning/housekeeping staff are also 100 percent. Don't expect your guests to understand or even consider this.

It is therefore essential to establish a workable check-in time for your guests and communicate this information to the best of your ability.

It's not as easy as you might think.

First of all, when determining an appropriate guest check-in time, you must consider everything you need to accomplish in order to be ready. So, in the summer when we're at 100 percent occupancy, our calculations begin with a check-out time. Using a worst-case scenario theory, i.e. excessively dirty cabins or damaged property, we have determined how much time it takes to prepare each unit for arriving guests. At our resort this not only includes cleaning and sterilizing kitchens and bathrooms and making up beds, vacuuming, dusting and window-cleaning, it also includes maintaining the grounds and picnic areas surrounding each cabin, trash collection and disposal, and tidying the massive beach/public areas. I must also consider the time it takes me to change out of my cleaning clothes and get the smell of bleach off my body to metamorphose from the cleaning lady to the check-in clerk. Even in a best-case scenario, i.e. cabins left in excellent condition, time is very limited when you need to accomplish everything in one day. Especially when you have a goal of perfection.

We initially determined an adequate time period was six hours. In our first years of operation, we therefore established our summer check-out and check-in times at 9:00 a.m. and 3:00 p.m. respectively. But for some reason—perhaps it was the hotel check-in scenario illustrated above—more often than not, guests showed up early and we simply weren't ready. So, we changed the check-in time to 3:30 to give us what turned out to be a necessary extra half-hour.

Guests still didn't get it. Apparently they only read the "3" on the reservation confirmation, and still showed up at 3:00. Or for some reason, they thought 3:30 actually meant 1:30 or 2:30.

Our last effort to try to alleviate the problem of early arrivals was to finally, change the check-in time to 4:00 p.m. We communicate this to guests on the phone during the initial reservation process, explaining that we can't accommodate early check-ins during the summer.

We reiterate it again in writing with a reservation confirmation and list of guidelines. We post it on our website, and we have a running light outside the resort office that flashes this information in bright red neon letters. We simply don't know what else to do. And in spite of all our efforts in all of these years of operation, it has been a given that some guests will—no matter what—show up early. Be prepared for this reality and don't let it upset you. Even if your hair is piled high in a messy bun, your clothes are stained, and you reek of cleaning supplies, try to smile at your guests and welcome them to your property. Have a plan to offer them comfort while you finish your chores and jump in the shower. You can eat your lunch later. Keep in mind that "perfection" is a wonderful goal, but it may be difficult to achieve every week. Sometimes you need to throw in the cleaning towel and proclaim your efforts as "good enough."

By the way, we tend to come up with a lot of mottos for our business while we're cleaning cabins, and one of our favorites is: "Sandy Point Resort—where good enough is."

Check-out time may often be sticky as well. You have to realize that guests have adapted to a slower, on-vacation pace, and the last thing they want to do is wakeup early, clean, pack, and get on the road back to reality. You will be flattered by their desire to "stay forever and keep living the dream life," for about three minutes. At 9:03 a.m., when you're parked in your golf cart outside of the cabins with all your new, clean bed linens, laundry baskets and buckets full of cleaning towels and potions, all you can think about is the clock ticking and the deadline you're facing.

In addition to communicating the check-out time in our printed reservation confirmation, on our website, in the guest services book in each cabin, on refrigerator notices and in framed information signs on the walls of each cabin, the last thing I do before handing guests keys to their cabins is to repeat it once again:

"Last but not least," I say with a smile, "and we hate to talk about your leaving us when you've only just arrived (smile again) . . . our check-out time on Saturday is 9:00 a.m. And we *do* enforce this time. So please respect the check-out time so we can once again, get the cabins as clean and ready for our next guests as we have for you today."

In the shoulder or off-seasons (May, September, October), we extend our check-out time until 11:00 a.m. We can also accommodate early check-ins, provided that we have advanced notice. Before and after the busy summer months guests may arrive as early as 2:00 p.m. Regardless of the season, resort guests are always welcome to use our disc golf course for free prior to their check-in time or after their check-out time, provided, of course, that they've officially checked out of the cabin.

Regarding check-out, once again I reference the hotel industry as most people know it from experience. If you stay at a hotel for more than one night, you expect the housekeeping staff to come by at some point to empty your trash, replace your towels and toiletries, makeup your bed and maybe even leave a mint on your pillow. Small inns as well as bed-and-breakfast operations are likely to provide these services as well.

When it's time to leave a hotel room, you may throw all your wet towels in a pile under the bathroom sink and leave your key on the nightstand, or bring it to the front desk; however, your only real job is to pack your things and go.

Sandy Point Resort, however, is what's known as a housekeeping facility with no American plan. According to the Municipal Property Assessment Corporation (MPAC), "a housekeeping cottage resort is a facility that provides, overnight, weekly or longer accommodations in a self-contained freestanding cottage structure (unit). Typically, the facility operator enters the unit only at the end of the guest's stay to clean and prepare the unit for the next guest." No American plan means "that the facility operator does not offer meals to their guests."

Because we do not go into the cabins on a daily basis to clean, we, in turn, ask and expect our guests to contribute to the overall housekeeping of the unit.

Early into our tenure as innkeepers we learned both how neatly people live and then again, how messy they can be as well. Both extremes make quite an impression. We have guests who leave the cabins so clean, they actually sparkle when we walk inside. These people make our job so pleasant I sometimes shed tears of gratitude (and I can't help but issue a thank-you note, email or text). Others make me want to shed tears for an entirely different reason.

Two or three years into the job, I discovered that certain consistent housekeeping tendencies of the cleaner/neater guests truly helped us with the time constraints on turnover day. For example, it saved a tremendous amount of time when guests stripped the sheets from the beds they used. You may not think it takes much time to strip a bed before making it up with clean sheets; however, if you figure 32 beds plus the possibility of futons and/or convertible sofas, and add the fact that some of these beds are "top bunks" (aka a great big pain in the *arse*), it makes a difference in not only time, but also physical labor.

So, rather than gamble with whether or not a guest would understand the meaning of "housekeeping facility" or live up to our hopeful expectations, I decided to be very specific about what we expected prior to departure. I typed up a "Before You Leave" list, laminated it and tacked it to the refrigerators of each cabin. At the time, I was teaching my young daughters the importance of asking for help when they needed it, and ultimately decided that it was okay for me to ask for help as well. Over the years I've shared this list with several other resort owners, innkeepers and property managers. Not all felt comfortable asking guests to comply; however, I have since stayed at housekeeping facilities that have asked far more, and in short, I have no regrets. For the most part, it works.

Guest Services

The comfort of your guests is paramount to the success of your operation. Since you've decided that you're a people person and you want to build a business that serves people, you must decide exactly what your services will entail. Keep in mind there will inevitably be a guest whom you simply cannot please. This is not your fault. It is only your fault if you fail to do your best to accommodate the *reasonable* expectations of your clientele. Note the key word is "reasonable." I know this will sound ridiculous, however, people will occasionally blame you for things as uncontrollable as the weather.

"You told us it was going to be a nice day on Thursday and so we rented a boat." Yes, more than once I've been accused of being a lousy meteorologist. As I result, I have learned not to offer weather forecasts as a guest service. In a place like Wisconsin where one regularly hears the old weather cliché, "if you don't like the weather, wait five minutes," which is a cliché because it is a FACT, it is best to keep mum when guests ask about the forecast. My only recourse has been to pull up websites and display the five-day outlook from services such as The Weather Channel, AccuWeather, and Weather

Welcome To Your Cabin

We hope you enjoy your stay at Sandy Point Resort

This is a housekeeping unit. Please respect it and be responsible for keeping it clean. Please note we do not offer cleaning or linen services. We expect you to leave the cabin the way you found it. To help keep our costs and rental rates down, please adhere to the following guidelines:

BEFORE YOU LEAVE

Remember check out time is NO LATER than 9:00 a.m.

1. Strip all used beds and compile the soiled sheets. DO NOT remove mattress pads. Leave blankets on bed.

2. Empty all waste cans in kitchens, bedrooms and bathrooms and use trash bins outdoors to store. Recycle appropriately. DO NOT LEAVE trash in cabin.

3. Wash, dry and put away all dishes and utensils.

4. If you have loaned anything to another cabin, please retrieve it and store in its proper place.

5. Vacuum all carpets.

6. Sweep all floors.

7. If you have made excess spills on stovetops, ovens, microwaves, or outdoor grills, please clean them.

8. Take out used coffee filters and discard.

9. Report all breakage or damage.

10. If you have used the fireplace, please clean out and dispose of ashes deep in the woods.

11. Return ALL furniture and appliances to original positions.

THANK YOU FROM THE COZZENS FAMILY

Underground, or show guests the National Weather Service radar, and have them draw their own conclusions.

It is highly important to have a general goal in mind when considering what you may and may not provide in terms of services and amenities; however, understand these decisions will most certainly evolve once you determine what you can and cannot handle.

We, for example, first envisioned our business would be to own and operate a bed-and-breakfast. It was because I like to decorate and clean and my husband/business partner likes to shop and cook. But since we were professional disc golfers, we also wanted to incorporate our passion for the sport/activity in how we made a living. We therefore made the decision to buy a property with enough land to build a disc golf course—and to do it in the Northwoods of Wisconsin where land was affordable at the time. Clearly, it changed the concept of our business plan from bed-and-breakfast to disc golf resort.

In the Northwoods, there was an abundance of housekeeping resorts and, Sandy Point, because it originally offered 40-acres, also provided the land on which we could build the course. So, what we ultimately delivered to our guests evolved from "bed-and-breakfast" to "bed-and-baskets" (aka disc golf course targets). Since each of our cabins provides full kitchen facilities and eating utensils, we decided to devote our time toward teaching disc golf and providing the equipment, rather than feeding our guests and providing the food.

When determining your guest amenities, ask yourself the following: Will you provide bed linens? And will you makeup the beds in advance of guests' arrival? Will you offer a sheet exchange in the event that one of their children wets the bed? Will you offer towels? (Bath towels? Kitchen towels? Beach towels?) How about personal hygiene items such as deodorant soap, hand soap, shampoo and conditioner? What types of housekeeping supplies are available in the units? Brooms? Vacuums? Grill brushes? If you provide boats with your cabins, as we do, do you also provide the state required life jackets?

You need to decide which amenities are included with the price of the rental rate and which you may or may not offer at a premium. We do offer boats, which are 14-foot rowboats exclusive to each cabin, but we charge extra for outboard motor rentals and the gas to run them. Guests who rent motors, which present an added liability factor, are required to not only fill out and sign a rental form and waiver, but also must succumb to operating instructions and a brief checkout procedure. We will help arrange for our guests to rent other boats and recreational equipment, but only by putting them in touch with reputable rental agencies. Guests may bring their own motors to put on the back of our boats and we do have gas/oil for sale on property.

In my memoir, *I'm Living Your Dream Life*, there's a chapter entitled "Frequently Asked Questions," where I listed not only the most frequently asked questions, but also the most unusual and even silly questions we had heard during the first ten years of operation. It's my daughters' favorite chapter, especially because even at the ages they were when the book was first published (seven and five), they'd heard these questions too. Ten years later, as teenagers, and ever since they started working in the front office/shop, they've probably heard each and every question in the book multiple times and could most likely double the list.

By the way, "what is disc golf?" continues to be the number one question we hear. Even though we were the sixth course to establish in the state of Wisconsin and at the time of this writing there are 152 Wisconsin courses registered with the Professional Disc Golf Association (PDGA), disc golf is still a novelty in many circles.

Answering guest questions is part of the service you provide. You may not wear the gold crossed-key pin of a traditional concierge; however, concierge services are most certainly required of you.

The word concierge comes from the French. It means "keeper of the keys," and yes, as owner/operator you do indeed keep the keys. And as I've already conveyed, I keep those keys until I'm paid! But your job isn't finished once you've gone from chief housekeeper or maintenance manager to front desk clerk. Throughout the duration of your guests' stay, you will be asked to reveal all you know about your property and the surrounding area. This requires being able to give explicit directions to every nearby town or attraction. You will draw or provide local maps, make restaurant recommendations, supply information on local recreational equipment rental operations, and steer people to the nearest, most reliable auto mechanic. Know where the nearest emergency room is located and/or the hours of the urgent care facility. Have a knowledge of what religious denominations area churches serve, and pay close attention to the times of Sunday mass for the Catholics, because most likely if someone asks about attending church while on vacation, it's a Catholic. I, by the way, was raised Catholic and our parents always took us to church on Sunday no matter where we were. Our mother sweetened the deal by telling us that each time we went to a new church, we were allowed to pray for three wishes. You might want to keep that one in your back pocket.

We have Internet service readily available in our front office and often resort to Google when we don't immediately know the answers. In each cabin, we provide a current Yellow Pages publication as well as a custom guest information book or binder. The binder includes everything from a brief history of the resort to a map of where things are located such as the life jackets, the firewood and the laundry facilities. It reiterates our trash and check-out time policies, as well as our policies about making future reservations. We list personal recommendations for area restaurants and attractions, and include a page entitled "What Is Disc Golf?" Our goal in creating the information binder was to answer most of the Frequently Asked Questions we've amassed over the years.

Trust, guests will still ask one or all of them at any time. Answer not with a sigh, but with a smile, and act as though it's the first time you've heard the question rather than the five-hundredth time.

Septic Systems

According to the U.S. Environmental Protection Agency (EPA), "nearly one in four households in the United States depends on an individual septic system or small community cluster system to treat wastewater." So, it's likely you're familiar with this type of onsite sewage system. But chances are, your guests will come from areas where their homes have connections to main sewage pipes provided by local governments or private corporations. It's certainly not the most glamorous system you need to understand, but as an innkeeper, toilets and everything about how they operate are highly relevant to your job. If, for example, you don't know what a ball cock is now, you will soon learn.

Have a reliable septic service person or company in your list of contacts. Not only will you need to maintain the systems by having them regularly pumped, our local government periodically requires that they be inspected for environmental safety. By the way, the water from our wells is also tested annually, a requirement from the state of Wisconsin. An inspector/tester comes to the property each Spring, shortly after we renew our annual business license.

Meanwhile, we provide our cabins with what we feel is an adequate toilet tissue supply for the duration of the guests' stay. Toilet paper is an amenity you simply must supply. We, however, don't replenish the supply if they run out. We indicate that if they need more toilet tissue, they'll need to supply it themselves. This is not to be stingy. This is our attempt to communicate the need to limit its use. Also, to educate our guests and perhaps even warn them about the system requirements, the following poem hangs above each toilet on the property:

Ode to the Septic Tank
All we folks with septic tanks
Give to you our heartfelt thanks
For putting nothing in the pot
That isn't guaranteed to rot.
Dental floss is bad, Kleenex too
Cigarette butts and hair combings are taboo.
No tampons or napkins,
Please use the basket!
There's a darn good reason
Why we ask it!

Over the years, several former guests have contacted me asking for the words to this poem. I didn't make it up, by the way. I read it in the bathroom of a small resort we toured prior to our first year of operation, and memorized it for future use. It was at a time when I had no idea that my dream life would include so many toilets.

Trash Policy
Since the summer of 2009, the cost of removing trash from our property has more than doubled. The first time the large increase, close to 75 percent, came unannounced in 2010, we contacted the waste management company to ask why. The company, one of only two choices in the area at the time, cited the rising cost of fuel and claimed that our volume had increased substantially. We couldn't argue the cost of fuel; however, we didn't understand the increased

volume. Not only had we not increased the number of rental units on property since 1995, overall occupancy levels were down. Further, traffic had decreased on the disc golf course by close to 20 percent. This was due in part to the economy, and also because a prolonged highway construction project made us inaccessible for a good portion of the high season. In the summer of 2011, it was the same situation with fuel prices, occupancy levels and disc golf traffic, and yet the trash collection bill went up another 50 percent. Ultimately, we discovered that our property had not been reevaluated in many years, and when a new manager came on board, she determined that we weren't being adequately charged to dispose of our recyclable materials. It was our bill to pay.

Remember when we used to get paid to turn in cans, glass and newspapers to recycling centers? The state of Wisconsin was at the forefront of the recycling movement in this country and when we purchased Sandy Point Resort, we communicated how recycling was mandatory according to Wisconsin state law. This was a bit of a foreign concept to many of our out-of-state guests. At some point during the last twenty years, waste management companies discovered there was no real money to be made by recycling—even though we are still required to do it. It's just that today it costs a lot of money to be environmentally responsible.

Look into your state and local laws regarding trash collection and recycling. If you live in a rural area with an accessible yet not always visible dumpster, be sure to either lock it or label it as private. This won't stop the bears and raccoons from trying to break in, but it may stop your neighbors from thinking it far more convenient than the local dump, and certainly less expensive than the local trash collector's pickup fees.

For our guests we provide the first kitchen trash bag and all waste baskets are also lined with recycled grocery bags. Outdoor disposal bins for each cabin are labeled "Trash Only" and "Recycling Only," and we provide a list of collectible recyclables. Outdoor bins are also lined with heavy-duty trash bags for easy removal and cleaning purposes. Tight-fitting lids are mandatory in order to withstand inevitable critter attacks. In some cases we have to fortify the lids with bungee cords. Those nocturnal raccoons certainly like to party and they're smart enough to wait until Friday nights when they know the bins are full.

Recreational Facilities

Use of all of our recreational facilities, the beach and swim area, playgrounds, recreation house and disc golf course, is included with the cost of the cabin rental. We provide basketballs for the basketball court, volleyballs for the volleyball court, golf discs for the disc golf course and old newspaper to wrap fish guts in the fish-cleaning house. Sand toys, swim-noodles, boat cushions and life jackets are stored at the beach and guests help themselves to their use.

In addition to a 14-foot rowboat exclusive to each cabin, we also provide paddleboats and a canoe for guests' use at no charge. Renting canoes and paddleboats, as well as other personal watercraft, is an income expansion possibility you may want to consider. When it comes to equipment rental, however, you must include in your projections the added liability potential and upkeep/maintenance expense.

The insurance company carrying your liability policy will periodically survey the property and pay particular attention to your recreational facilities and policies. If you have a beach and swimming area, for example, and there's no lifeguard on duty, this information must be posted. If you have a tripping hazard like a large rock or exposed root near your swing-set, you will be required to remove it.

If any of your facilities has limited hours of operation, post this information clearly. Our recreation house hours, for instance, coincide with our established "quiet hours," which are 10:00 p.m. until 8:00 a.m. Trust, a rousing and competitive game of ping pong can keep the whole property hopping to the wee hours if you don't establish and enforce quiet hours.

Because we offer a recreational activity or attraction on our property aside from our cabin rental operation, our disc golf course requires a good deal of special attention to the established policies and procedures. This may be the case for you if you intend for your innkeeping business to include a recreational attraction or a bar, restaurant or meetings and banquet facilities.

Our disc golf course attracts a very different customer than the typical suburban family on vacation. (It also requires entirely different advertising and marketing techniques). Treating it as a satellite business—a disc, if you will, flying around the business as a whole—we need to enforce a different set of rules with customers who are on property strictly to play disc golf.

Please note we do allow and encourage our resort guests (i.e. cabin renters) to play the course at no charge. It has been our mission since the onset of creating the world's first disc golf resort to teach people about the sport and how to play it. The success of our mission has indeed paid off in revenue, because the more people we turn onto disc golf, the more enthusiasts emerge, who not only return to play the course but also contribute to our retail operation by buying golf discs and other disc golf related products.

It's because our course is so expansive (27 holes as opposed to most courses, which are 18 holes), well designed, unique and even famous, that there is a great deal of demand by disc golfers from around the world to play it. We therefore opened it to the public and charge a $5 green fee to play. The $5 charge is good for all-day play and includes the use of rental golf discs. Yes, we still charge the fee if players bring their own discs. Kids under the age (repeat: UNDER the age) of 12 are free. If you're 12, you pay. We have to repeat this nearly every day. And because we were one of the world's first pay-to-play facilities and a great majority of the world's disc golf courses are in public parks that do not charge admittance fees, even though we've been doing it for nearly 20 years, the idea of paying a green fee still upsets some players. It sometimes upsets them even further when they learn that the course green fee does not include the use of our beach and waterfront facilities. We don't mind if golfers take a look or tour the grounds after their round, as it inevitably leads to future cabin rentals, but nearly every day we must reiterate that the beach is for resort guest use only. We do offer a picnic area and grill just outside of our pro shop, and provide a clean public restroom with running water. We further invite disc golfers to visit the Wisconsin Disc Golf Hall of Fame, which is located on property in the recreation house.

Office Hours

My friend and colleague, Jenny Gibson, is the third generation owner/operator of Black's Cliff Resort in Hazelhurst, Wisconsin a Northwoods resort since 1918. We first met at a shop in the town of Minocqua, the island city located between our respective towns. She happened to recognize me from the photo featured on the back of my first book, *I'm Living Your Dream Life: The Story of a Northwoods Resort Owner,* and she introduced herself. She was immediately likable—definitely a people person. Having grown up at Black's Cliff, she ultimately inherited the job of owner/operator, and she related to our *Dream Life* story probably more than anyone.

"Oh my gosh," she said, "I could have inserted my and Troy's names for yours and Mike's at any point and it would be the exact same story!"

In particular, she cited an incident I relayed about a woman off the street who one early morning walked into my kitchen to ask about the property for sale next door. At the time I happened to be in my nightgown and my boob was exposed because I was nursing my baby! Even though the intruding woman had entered our front office, which was attached to our home at the time, to get into my kitchen, she opened a door with a big sign reading: "PRIVATE." When I informed her that she was in a private home, she was unapologetic and once again asked about the real estate.

Jenny tells a story about literally getting caught with her pants down. The same thing happened to her when an intruder (or "no-knocker" as she calls them) walked into her home, mistaking it for the office. Lo and behold, he discovered her in the bathroom taking care of business, and because she was in a hurry and no one was home, oops, she had left the bathroom door open.

Last I heard from Jenny on the subject, she was in the process of finally building a new front office, and it will most certainly be de-tached from her home.

In this business you will give up a good deal of your privacy by sharing your home/property with your customers. You really won't understand what that truly feels like until you get caught in some state of undress. But it won't need to go to this extreme before you realize it. This is why it's important to have an office separate from your home. If this isn't possible, find a way to make the door leading to your private living quarters invisible or inaccessible.

Also, set office hours. If you don't set office hours, your doorbell will ring at any time of the day or night. It will ring before your morn-ing shower, or the moment you sit down to dinner or a movie, or after you turn-in for the evening and lay your head on the pillow.

We set our office hours from ten to five daily, and stay open until 7:00 p.m. on Saturday evenings during the summer in order to ac-commodate late arrivals and tend to the extra needs of guests when they first arrive. We make it very clear that we are available outside of office hours in case of emergency; however, sometimes "emergency" must be defined. Guests getting locked out of their cabins certainly qualifies; however, if someone simply wants to buy a candy bar, well you get the point.

To sum up the topic of policies and procedures, I have tried to include the obvious as well as the more obscure topics and issues that are less familiar to those who aren't experienced in the industry. Our policies and procedures continue to develop with each passing season. For example, firewood, fireworks and fish guts policies have all either recently changed or still need to be worked out.

• Firewood was once free at Sandy Point Resort. But we simply couldn't keep up with the demand. In other words, there was a lot of labor involved with no financial payoff. We still keep our seasoned/split firewood in a centrally-located hut, but now we charge $5 per wheelbarrow. Supply has maintained consistent, yet demand (now that it's no longer free) has gone down. In other words, it's now a more manageable issue, and in the summer of 2011, this hot commodity brought in a total of $450. Guests pay for firewood on an honor system—inserting cash into a locked box located on the hut itself—and I'm happy to report that our guests are honorable people. The definition of "wheelbarrow full," however, has a wide range of interpretation. Some truly get their five-bucks worth by piling logs so high they fall off like a trail of bread crumbs all the way back to their personal fire pits.

• Fireworks are another burning issue—pun intended. They are illegal nearly everywhere and yet there are loopholes. In the state of Wisconsin, the general rule is if the device "explodes or leaves the ground," a permit is required. So, things like sparklers and snakes are okay, but roman candles and bottle rockets are not. Because we live adjacent to an Indian Reservation (The Lac du Flambeau Band of Lake Superior Chippewa), where not all state laws either apply or have the same restrictions, local fireworks stands pop up only a couple miles away from our resort each summer, and they offer plenty of fireworks that both leave the ground and explode. If guests only set off fireworks on the 4th of July, it would be a more manageable situation; however, for some reason—as we discover during every week of every summer—people on vacations tend to think every day is the 4th of July.

• Fish guts and what to do with them is a widely discussed topic among Northwoods resort owners. Whether one chooses to wrap them in newspaper and add to the dumpster, bury them or tote them far into the woods, these stinking, slimy disgusting things are part of the business. The number one rule we convey to resort guests is that fish may not be cleaned inside the cabins. I promise you, no cleaning chore is more difficult and infuriating than scraping fish scales from kitchen countertops! It's like trying to remove drops of dried Super Glue. This rule is listed on a framed document in each cabin, plus above each kitchen sink it appears in ALL CAPS on a florescent, blaze orange label, which is brighter than a gun-season hunting getup. Yes, sometimes you have to shout!

We provide a fish-cleaning hut near the lake and ask guests to wrap guts in newspaper and dispose into a labeled bin until we can periodically remove them. The thing we don't like and don't exactly know how to communicate is that we prefer it if our guests don't import fish guts from fish caught in other lakes. As described above, trash collection and maintenance is a big expense for us and we simply don't want guests to import it in from the outside. You know those signs at gas stations where you often see people cleaning out all their fast food containers and other waste from their cars while pumping gas? They read: "No Household Garbage." By the way, this happens all the time in our disc golf course parking lot, where golfers regularly clean out their cars and put trash in the bins on our first tee. When I see it happening, I can't help but ask the person doing it why he wants to bring me his trash? It's just so rude! Anyway, as far as excessive fish guts are concerned, I have it in my mind to paint a new sign for the fish-cleaning hut that reads something like: "Fish Not Caught Near—Don't Clean Here." We once saw graffiti on a sea wall in Santa Cruz, California presumably sprayed by local surfers: "Don't Live Near—Don't Surf Here." Just like a territorial surfer, I guess there's no such thing as a resort owner hanging loose over things like fish guts.

Chapter 6:
A Day In The Life

Prior to visiting Sandy Point Resort for the first time, my dear friend Anne Beaver asked me to give her a detailed description of a day in my life at the resort. I hesitated before responding, because when you have a job that requires you to be on duty seven days per week, not every day is the same. There is, however, a fairly predictable routine, especially during the summer when we follow a Saturday-to-Saturday pattern.

For those of you who have regular, Monday through Friday, nine-to-five jobs, do you know that feeling you sometimes get on a Sunday night particularly after an either restful or eventful and fun weekend? It's a feeling that makes you want to sigh, knowing there'll be a change the next day, which is neither restful nor particularly fun. In our business, that feeling comes on Friday night when we face a full turnover on any given Saturday.

We have learned to take the summers one Saturday at a time.

In order to get a jumpstart on the Saturday process, after we close the office/shop at 5:00 p.m. on Friday, I prepare all the necessary supplies. In our massive storage area where we keep all the cleaning supplies and bed linens, we have a large, uncluttered worktable. There we keep a box of kitchen trash bags and a black Sharpie marker. The first thing I do is pull bags and use the Sharpie to write cabin numbers on each. I then pull sets of sheets from the linen storage, organized by cabin numbers, and store them in the bags. Because of limited time for turnover, it is essential that each bed on property has at least two sets of sheets designated for it exclusively. You should also have extra pillowcases for spare pillows and a stash of extra blankets and quilts, and mattress pads in all sizes.

Each bag of sheets is then placed in a plastic laundry basket, which also carries a cabin number label. Since we offer beds in a variety of sizes—twin, double, queen, king and California king—and our sheets have a lot of flavor (i.e. different colors and patterns) rather than standard, hotel-industry white, it's important that we keep them organized. I may know the particular colors and patterns that go on each bed in each cabin, but I am the only one. The rest of our housekeeping staff simply hasn't committed sheet-knowledge to memory. I therefore have laminated photos of the sheets that are used for each cabin on display above the worktable. I have also used my handy Sharpie marker to label each sheet with bed size and cabin number. In spite of how well I know the sheets, it's still easy to confuse full size sheets with queen size. Sometimes I need to double-check the label.

We do our own laundry at Sandy Point Resort and I believe we are unique in keeping laundry as a D.I.Y. chore. Many of our colleagues farm out this process; however, I honestly don't mind it and want to pay close attention to any stains or tears in the bed linens. I especially take pride in my ability to fold fitted sheets. Ask anyone who knows me how perfect they are. (In my job as innkeeper, sheets play an even bigger role than toilets). Meanwhile, depending on your location, the going rate for laundry service including washing and "mangling" or folding, is approximately a dollar per pound. And a set of folded king-sized sheets weighs about four-and-a-half pounds. (I don't know whether or not they weigh more when crumpled and soiled—but probably). So, do the math, consider your laundry equipment and septic systems, and your time, and budget accordingly.

After organizing the sheets I turn to the cleaning products. We are always long on cleaning supplies such as toilet bowl cleaner, bathroom cleaner, bleach, orange cleaner, Windex and Swiffer juice (floor cleaner) and Swiffer pads. We purchase most of our cleaning supplies in bulk from Sam's Club. Even though it's located about 80 miles away in Wausau, in order to capitalize on the savings this warehouse club store provides for the cost of an annual membership fee, we plan periodic shopping trips and fill the truck with necessary supplies. Toilet paper definitely takes up the most room.

We are constantly approached by either guests in the cleaning products business (everything from Amway to Organic—aka expensive—products), or through phone, mail and drop-by solicitors, who are trying to obtain our cleaning supply business. We've experimented with various cleaning products over the years and are now comfortable with what we regularly use. Most are readily available, commercial brands. We use the worktable to refill individual spray bottles from super-sized jugs and then stock two plastic totes with complete cabin cleaning kits. We also have a massive supply of cleaning towels and store all clean towels in a green, five-gallon bucket. Green = Clean. A spare white, five-gallon bucket starts empty; however, on Saturday it is soon filled with the used/dirty towels. Cloth cleaning towels, by the way, are far more economical than paper towels. Plus, in spite of having to wash them each week, they're still better for the environment.

Other supplies to prepare are bathroom rugs, toilet tissue, and plastic bags to line all small wastebaskets. For this we recycle our grocery bags. The plastic bags we use to store and deliver new sheets to each cabin, ultimately serves as the liner for the cabin's kitchen trash container.

Getting the cabin and cleaning supplies together the night before our big turnover enables us not only to relax a little more, but also allows us to spring into action the moment a cabin is vacated on Saturday morning. Occasionally, guests leave early and we will, by all means, devote our Friday evenings toward turning over any and all vacant cabins, just to make Saturday a less demanding day.

Saturdays, in a word, suck. Sorry, but it's true. There's nothing more we can do but prepare as much as we can in advance, then dive in and dedicate ourselves toward doing a good job from start-to-finish. Because we've been lucky in attracting such wonderful guests to the resort, more often than not, our cabins are left in good shape. When it's a straightforward turnover, the job of cleaning really isn't so bad. In fact, particularly when our teenagers are in a good mood, it's actually fun. We talk about funny things that happened with the guests during the previous week, rock-out to music, and even listen to audio books. In fact, I listened to five of the seven Harry Potter books while cleaning cabins, and to this day I cannot make certain beds without somehow thinking I'm in a room at Hogwarts.

With a cabin cleaning staff of four, we divide the chores. One does kitchens, one does bathrooms and two do beds plus vacuuming, dusting and windows. Our full-time caretaker, who would be the fifth staff member, first grooms the lakefront and prepares the boats, then moves onto trash duty and the picnic areas of each cabin. We all take turns manning the pro shop and dealing with visitors who drop by to tour the grounds for potential future bookings. We'd prefer to handle visitors when not in cleaning mode; however, we simply can't keep anyone from coming to the property on Saturday. Often we have personal visitors staying for the weekend, and they help out by manning the shop. We've also had a long chain of nephews stay for prolonged periods over the years. We affectionately refer to them as "whipping boys," and they do pretty much anything we ask them to do. We generally don't have to whip them.

Once the cabins are cleaned they are ready for a final inspection. According to the Family, Career and Community Leaders of America, a final inspection "makes the difference between just cleaning the room and doing a professional job." Often during final inspections, we replace things like missing forks or spoons or broken glasses, or we find cleaning products we may have left behind. Occasionally we discover issues we may have overlooked, like fingerprints on glass doors or an unlined wastebasket.

Finally, with the cabins inspected and locked, we turn our attention to the outbuildings. We clean the recreation house, public bathroom and laundry facility, and make sure the firewood hut is stocked.

Our cabin cleaning staff hasn't always consisted of just the four of us. When we first purchased Sandy Point Resort, we didn't have children. I used to joke that I needed to give birth to a sixteen year-old boy in order to help out with the chores. With the exception of the whipping boys, I never got the sixteen year-old boy, but these days, our two teenage girls are definitely an asset. They do an excellent job—caring almost as much as we do about the property—and we pay them an hourly rate for all chores they perform around the resort. They each turn-in a weekly time sheet. They also advertise and provide a babysitting service, for which guests pay them directly.

Prior to Willow and Camille joining the cleaning staff, we hired outside help. Depending upon the size of the property you develop, unless you are adamant about keeping it as a mom-and-pop operation, there is a possibility of either the need or the desire to take on employees. And I wish you good luck with that.

I dare say that any business owner will claim that "good help is hard to find." You've probably heard that old saw even more often than any weather cliché. Again, it's because it's true. If your innkeeping operation is in a vacation or resort community, there is a high demand for housekeepers, and any help at all may be hard to find. We've tried high school students and college students, some of whom were unreliable and occasionally hung-over, and then one person who charged $18-20 per hour and ultimately only made beds. Claiming asthma, she wouldn't dust or sweep, and by her last year with us she had developed allergies to all the cleaning products as well. The good news is that she was fast, always showed up on time, and she did a good job on the beds—except for the top bunks, which she wouldn't makeup due to vertigo.

Thank goodness, our girls grew up and joined the cleaning staff.

Rule of thumb when it comes to hiring help: NO ONE will care about your property and your business as much as you do. This is not meant to imply that it's impossible to find adequate help. If you do find someone who does a great job and truly embraces the work, reward that person generously and hold on as best as you can.

Some may categorize the job of cleaning person as unskilled labor, but I beg to differ. As a commercial operation, cleaning our cabins requires a professional touch, performed with great care and basic knowledge and understanding of the supplies used to accomplish this job. For example, the state of Wisconsin mandates that kitchen utensils be sterilized with a bleach solution each time the unit is turned over.

"Utensils shall be effectively sanitized by being submerged in a hypochlorite solution with a chlorine concentration continuously maintained at 100 parts per million, or another approved sanitizing solution which shall be used at the concentration at which tested and approved by the department."[2]

You must know how to handle and dilute bleach, and specifically understand that it should never be mixed with other cleaners containing ammonia, as this will form a deadly gas.

---

[2] Wisconsin Government Code, Department of Health Services, Section DHS 197.12.

The state has several requirements for annual license renewal. Each year, in order to keep our business license active, a representative from the state Department of Health Services inspects the cabins and grounds. The inspector is usually an avid intern or fresh college graduate, who likes to cross each T and dot each i.

In addition to the cooking and eating utensils, the state inspector checks the made-up beds as well. Did you know that sheets must be pulled over the top of the blanket and the fold is to measure 13-inches? This is the minimum requirement to keep the blanket from touching the guest, which thereby enables you to not have to wash the blanket each time you change the sheets. Another method is called "triple sheeting," which is a bed-making procedure that uses a fitted sheet and two flat sheets surrounding the blanket. We opt for the 13-inch fold rather than use an additional sheet in order to limit the linen supply and the bulk of the weekly laundry. Regardless, all blankets must be checked weekly, and periodically laundered or exchanged.

For the innkeeper, bed-making is not only a skill, it's an art. We have to meet state health requirements and also make each bed look beautiful and inviting.

As the state continually finds ways to achieve the goal of reducing "exposure to environmental and safety hazards in public lodging and recreational areas," there are often new requirements, which we discover during inspection. For instance, three years ago we had to install smoke and carbon monoxide detectors in each bedroom, which were in addition to the detectors already installed in the living areas. (That was about a $400 expense for which we hadn't budgeted). From that point forward, the inspector's job includes testing the nine-volt batteries, which we need to replace annually. Oh, and the local fire marshal comes by each spring as well, to not only test the smoke detectors, but also to make sure the fire extinguishers required for each unit have been inspected, recharged and tagged.

After cleaning, I immediately jump in the shower. And if there's time to eat prior to guest arrival and the check-in procedure gets underway, I chow down on a cheeseburger from Musky Jack's. Musky Jack's, an area bar and grill open since 1929, is located about five miles down the road, and boasts "Awesome Burgers" on its outdoor sign. It's our usual Saturday fare, and after a late lunch, we tend to skip dinner on Saturday evening.

Our front office, which we built in 1999, doubles as a shop, where we carry golf discs and other disc golf related items, as well as jewelry and unique Northwoods souvenirs and gifts. Between checking in guests, I inevitably deal with shop customers and people who come to play disc golf. My station is at the glass counter behind the cash register.

Arriving guests always get priority on Saturday afternoon. Since most of them are repeat customers, it's an unpretentious process to first greet them warmly and then have them fill out the registration form and sign the liability waiver. They pay the cabin rental fees and all required taxes—sales tax and room tax rates vary from state to state and it's important to keep track of the taxes you collect, and pay the state department of revenue either monthly or quarterly, depending on the requirements. Once I receive payment in full, I give guests their keys and off they go. It's a longer procedure with new guests.

By process of elimination and knowing who is expected on property, it is usually easy to greet new guests by name. If you have them at hello, chances are you'll be able to hold their attention through the duration of your check-in procedure. State law requirements for licensing your lodging establishments inlcudes official guest registration. Guests must register their "true names and addresses," and in Wisconsin, we need to keep them on file for at least a year. For security purposes and to meet our stipulation that all vehicles must be registered, we also require license plate numbers of all cars on property. The registration process does include more than obtaining guest information. You must provide information as well. And during this process, keep in mind that there are few things more annoying than a gabby check-in clerk when you've just driven five or six hours with a car full of antsy kids and grocery bags full of freshly purchased perishables, and all you want to do is start your vacation.

As innkeeper, it's important to communicate the necessary policies and procedures that will ultimately make your guests' stay easier on both of you; however, it's more important to make it brief. In my experience with new guests, I have the full attention of about 50 percent. With the other half, I feel their impatience and indifference to my instructions as their bodies are still rumbling from the road. So, I suggest you just do your best and keep smiling. Don't take it personally. Road trips may be a great deal less complicated than flying these days; however, many people are stressed by traveling no matter what form of transportation they use. Your job is to help them leave the road behind, and ease into a period of relaxation.

I get a special kick out of teenagers, by the way, who usually stand with a hand-on-a-hip and cast an irreverent glare in my direction, like it's MY fault they've been forced to leave their friends back home and go on vacation with their family. Sometimes I'll give the teenager the key, tell her she's in charge, and then after she's left the office, assure her parents that she'll be their little girl again the moment she puts on her swimsuit and jumps off the water trampoline. There's something about the water of Squaw Lake that serves as a baptismal or rejuvenation function, bringing out the child in everyone.

When 7:00 p.m. comes, and it comes in a hurry due to the volume of activity, it's time to turn out the lights and go inside. Saturday night is never a time to roam the grounds or try to steal a few peaceful moments at the lake. There are two reasons for this. One, I'm exhausted and probably won't be at my best when dealing with guests on property. Two, I like to give guests who've freshly arrived the chance to acclimate in their own manner. They don't need the owner hovering over them as they explore and discover everything about the property. If they have questions, most likely they'll be answered by reading the information binder in their cabin, or they can simply find me in the morning.

A note on "roaming the grounds:" It may be before or after your established office hours, but trust that whenever you are visible to guests, you should consider yourself available. Even when you're sitting alone at the end of a dock, sweating from a long run in the woods and plugged into your iPod, someone will inevitably sit down next to you and ask you about how big the lake is and how long you've owned the place.

I feel like I am not just visible at Sandy Point, I am *intensely* visible. (It's one reason I don't parade around in a bikini). The key is to be prepared for these interruptions to your moments of solitude, accept them, and keep trying to find ways to get them. Otherwise, the job may drive you crazy. Running works for me. So do the late afternoon/early evening escapes on the boat.

On every day but Saturday, the routine is far more pleasant and relaxing for this innkeeper. I usually get up and go for a run, and then clean up and get into the office/shop by 10:00. Recording the previous days credit card settlement and sales is the first chore and it must be done on a daily basis. I never let these things pile up. Taking care of the daily bookkeeping is as sacred and constitutional as a morning prayer or a morning run.

If it's not busy in the shop, like on rainy days when disc golf traffic is down, we lock the front door and guests/customers are instructed to ring the bell for service. If we see golfers or shoppers pull up or resort guests walk up, we immediately return to the shop. If we're inside the house, we hear the bell, as it rings (loudly) in our home. Someone attends to business at once. We all take turns.

When resort guests ring the bell, they most often want to get a movie (DVD), a candy bar, or change for a twenty. Early in the week, they ask to use our compressor to blow up innertubes or float toys. Occasionally they need help maneuvering their trailers or help figuring out how to use the television remote. Sometimes they just want to chat or, of course, shop. Customers off the street are predominately there to play disc golf. We have a slot on the wall for green fees, but we also supply golf discs, score cards and give lessons upon request. Mike and I spend a lot of time on Hole #1 giving forehand and backhand throwing demonstrations.

Because I also spend a lot of time camped on the front porch of our house where I can see the driveway, the main walkways, and the lake, between customers, I pass the time there either reading or indulging in various crafts projects. In addition to making jewelry, I also like to use birch bark to make baskets, canoe ornaments and switch plate covers, which we sell in the shop. I spent another recent summer turning our massive collection of Coke bottle caps into hanging crosses. We have a vintage Coke machine on the front porch of our shop. It's the kind that takes quarters only, and after inserting them into the coin slot, a "Have a Coke!" light turns on, and you pull out the bottle. A bottle opener is on the machine and the caps drop into a container inside the machine. I promise you, the Coke machine is not something we consider to be an income expansion option. It makes us no money. The product (8 and 12 oz. bottles) is expensive, and the machine needs constant maintenance and attention. But it's a Sandy Point novelty and each day kids run to the porch with coins jingling in their pockets, and claim it to be one of the coolest things they've ever seen.

Busy or slow, my favorite time of day is at 5:00 on any given week-day. During the summer, the days are long way up north, and there's plenty of daylight left to enjoy the lake. Most of our resort guests and other lake residents have begun preparing for dinner, which means we often have either the disc golf course, or the beach and all 785 acres of the lake to ourselves. Squaw Lake is a nice, big lake and it's not on a chain. This is a key selling point for us because we tell prospective resort guests that there are no watercraft restrictions and there's lots of water to explore with very little boat traffic. The only truly busy times on Squaw Lake are around the 4th of July and then again during the first week of August, which is a prime vacation week. This is because it's the week just after summer school has ended and just before autumn sports programs begin.

If it's a warm, calm night and the water is smooth, we waterski. If it's windy or chilly, we take out the "tooner," aka the pontoon boat, which we have named "Dream Life." We bring along chardonnay for Mommy, Diet Coke with Lime for Daddy and Gatorade or Arnold Palmers for the girls, along with cheese and crackers for all.

When we pull away from the shore and commune with the pair of loons that annually nests near our shore, and spot the American bald eagles soaring overhead, we marvel at how beautiful and peaceful the shores of Sandy Point Resort appear from a distance. Even after all these years, we can't believe it's ours. In these moments, we don't think about things like diluting bleach and cleaning cabins. We think we're living a dream life.

Chapter 7:
Expecting the Unexpected

We've met many colleagues in the innkeeping business over the past two decades and I can't stress enough the importance of having allies and advisors. We've received an enormous benefit from joining a local association called the Minocqua Area Resorts Association (MARA), which formed in the early 2000s. MARA consists of mostly family-owned and operated resorts like Sandy Point, but it also includes area bed-and-breakfasts and other types of lodging facilities. It's a low-key association that holds meetings only two times per year. The cost for membership is only $50 annually and the bulk of promotion is done via a very well-designed website.

Without a doubt, the most beneficial aspect of membership in this association is the relationships we've formed with other resort owners, especially when it comes to referrals when trying to fill last-minute cancellations. It may be difficult to find the time, particularly during your high season, but make a point of getting to know as many other innkeepers as you can by either association memberships or by attending meetings of the local Chamber of Commerce or Area Business Association.

The people from whom we purchased Sandy Point were the first innkeepers we got to know well. Part of our arrangement when negotiating the sale was that they agreed to spend time training us and sharing some of their operating methods. They had owned Sandy Point for eight years and were very knowledgeable about the idiosyncrasies of the property. Their input and the reservations they had made a year in advance played a key role in enabling us to get through that first summer of 1993.

When you purchase an existing innkeeping property, by all means, obtain some type of education about how the property operates. You may have already had years of experience or even a degree in hotel/motel management, but you cannot discount the value of gathering intimate knowledge specific to the property at hand. Not all septic systems and well pumps operate in the same manner. And you may not have thought about handling your reservation system in the way that has worked for the property owner prior to your takeover. State-of-the-art technology develops and changes at a rapid pace, and while it's your duty to keep up with the changes, you may not always be in a position to evolve with the times. First find out what works, and then determine how you can work it.

We, for example, still use the paper reservation book with the same format as the previous owners. What we added was the online calendar, which serves as an informative tool for potential guests and a cross-reference check for us. I've considered using an online reservation system, where guests could actually book cabins and pay deposits via the Internet, but I don't want to take away the personal touch from the process. I want potential guests to hear my voice—to understand this is truly a family-owned and operated property—and further, I want to get to know them a little bit too. After all, in spite of all our efforts to maintain some degree of privacy, there's a small chance that they might walk in on me in my underwear! Further, double-booking is perhaps the biggest mistake I can make as an inn-keeper, and I'm afraid that an online system might cause trouble in the event that our computer crashes, or Internet service is down for any length of time. It happens in urban and suburban areas, trust it also happens in the woods!

On the subject of power outages, not only did we not expect that electrical outages would be a regular occurrence, at first we didn't understand the degree to which we relied on electrical power in order to have a successful operation. I can't speak for all rural areas across the country but I can explain that in the Northwoods, power outages are often the result of storm damage. For the most part, power lines are not buried and a storm with high winds and/or lightening strikes causes tree branches to take out the lines. When the power goes out, it has a blanket effect on the property as a whole, and usually the entire north and east ends of the lake as well.

When the power goes out and I'm sitting in the dark, I check my wristwatch and expect to hear from the first guests within about five minutes. "The power's out in our cabin," they say. Sometimes they add things like, "I've got meat in the fridge that is in danger of going bad." We then expect a parade of individual guests to report this problem one-at-a-time. All we can do is thank them for bringing it to our attention, and assure them we'll take care of the situation to the best of our ability.

If it's apparent the outage is more than a flicker or that it may have a significant duration, we report the incident to our power company, Price Electric, which is some 40 miles away. In our experience, the company knows about the outages in advance of our call 50 percent of the time. Price Electric is an electricity distribution cooperative with six substations and over 1,800 miles of distribution lines. It does not generate any electric power. Due in part to the large, rural area it serves, it may take anywhere from an hour or three or even twenty-four before the problem is solved. If it's not a problem at one of the substations, sometimes it may take hours to merely locate the site of the culprit fallen tree. As a matter of record, our longest outage after a particularly destructive area storm was five days.

For your guests' comfort, the sake of the meat in their refrigerators, and your ability to operate either a retail or restaurant operation, have a backup power system in place. If and when our power is out for more than an hour, we resort to gasoline-powered generators. We have several—enough to power up each cabin as well as the office/shop—and it's labor intensive to get them operating. Keep in mind, when getting them into action, we often have to work in the dark *and* the rain. This is why we wait until we're sure the outage is actually significant before resorting to their use. The challenge is not only in supplying all the generators with gas (which hopefully we have an ample supply in storage), but we also have to get into the cabins and manipulate the breaker boxes. We must inform guests of the need to power down and avoid using things like microwaves and hairdryers. Inevitably, some type of electronic component or piece of equipment blows out during the ordeal and needs to be replaced.

The lesson? Have a spare *everything*. Have extra coffee makers,

VCR/DVD players, televisions and boom boxes. Have spare gasoline and even have a spare generator because they can be pesky creatures from time-to-time and not want to fire-up. And in the meantime, have sparc candles, which you can give to your guests to use until the lights come back on.

When lightening strikes your well pump, on the other hand, it's not exactly practical to have a spare well pump on hand. This happened to us in 1995—totally unexpected, of course—and we had no choice but to replace the pump. Thankfully, it was covered by insurance. Things like water heaters have a shelf life as well, but they're not prone to calamities like lightening strikes. Usually when a water heater malfunctions, a simple solution is to replace the heating element. If you're having trouble with the pilot light it might be something like a thermal coupler. Whatever the trouble, expect to learn a lot about basic household appliances and how to fix them. You don't want to call in and pay for a pro unless it's a last resort. There's a great website, "How to Repair Anything," (http://www.howtorepairany-thing.net); and every resort owner should have a copy of the Reader's Digest book, *Fix-It-Yourself Manual.*[3]

During our first year we inherited several guests from the previous owners. As part of our initial training session, the sellers went through the reservation book for the upcoming summer and pointed out a few characteristics to expect. "They're always late with the deposit," for example; or "That guy charges his boat into the shore and lifts up the motor at the last minute;" or "these people will leave the cabin cleaner than they found it." They were spot-on for each of these proclamations. Overall, however, they were quite guarded about telling us anything detrimental or gossipy. And after our first season, when we shared with them a story or two of some particularly destructive guests, they knowingly nodded their heads. "We'd been wanting to get rid of them for years," they said. I remember laughing first and then chastised them for not warning us. "We wanted you to find out some things about this business on your own," they said.

Boy, did we.

During our first meeting with the previous owner, my husband

---

[3] *New Fix-It-Yourself Manual: How to Repair, Clean, and Maintain Anything and Everything In and Around Your Home*; Readers Digest, June, 1996; 448 pages.

asked him why he was selling the place. His answer was immediate: "I'm tired of people wrecking my stuff." Because of this we expected that things would break; however, we didn't understand or realize how we'd feel about people "wrecking" things to the degree they actually did.

I think we had to replace our basketball hoop five times in the first five years due to people hanging on it. One week we had to replace every single drinking glass in one of the cabins due to, we suppose, breakage. Screens and screen doors require weekly attention and/or repair and Teflon or non-stick pots and pans need to be replaced constantly because people stir their noodles with a fork rather than a plastic or wooden spoon. We put two and even three cutting boards in each kitchen to try to discourage guests from slicing vegetables directly on the countertops, and you'd be amazed at how many spoons and forks we go through each summer. They seem to just disappear. We keep around plenty of spare plugs and parts for the paddleboats as we see them abused and flooded week after week. One of the more upsetting and memorable incidents was when a kid with a Coke fresh from our vintage Coke machine decided to pour the contents into the pockets of our pool table.

Question: Who does that kind of thing?
Answer: Your customers.
Solution: Learn to expect the unexpected.

My friend, Jenny, of Black's Cliff Resort, once told me she looked out her kitchen window and saw guests dragging an antique wooden table across a dirt road with the intention of taking it from one cabin to another. Another Northwoods resort owner related an instance when guests poured gasoline on the logs of an indoor fireplace and basically blew up the cabin. The owner of a small family resort in Washington state wrote to me after reading *I'm Living Your Dream Life* and related a story about a couple who once had full blown sex on the beach in the middle of the afternoon in front everyone. Another pair of long-term and seasoned Northwoods resort owners, Denny and Sue Robertson of the historic Dillman's Sand Lake Lodge in Lac du Flambeau, whom I'm pleased to call my friends, once told me about a guest who cut down a carved totem pole on property and used it as firewood. They definitely didn't see that one coming.

One of the oddest things we've had happen was when a guest decided to remove and take all of the middle door hinges from the doors inside his cabin. We didn't immediately discover the missing hinges so we never determined who did it. We also can't imagine why someone felt the need to take them or for what they may have been used.

Guests also say some of the weirdest and most unexpected things. Not that long ago we hosted a guest who had planned to stay for four days. After day two, she charged into the office/shop and pushed her way to the counter where two disc golf customers were already standing. Interrupting our conversation about the latest and greatest disc golf disc for sale, she shouted at me. "The weather stinks! The fishing's terrible! And my mother and husband are fighting!" She then slammed her key on the glass counter top and proclaimed, "We're OUT of here!" She turned, walked out the front door and then slammed it so hard that products fell off the shelves and display golf discs fell off the walls. The customers I'd been dealing with looked at me with dropped jaws. "Wow," they said. "Did that really just happen?" We all had a good laugh, but I was a little embarrassed. I was also scared to go inside the cabin she had just so adamantly abandoned, thinking it might be trashed, especially with all that fighting her husband and mother were supposedly doing. But that wasn't the case. The cabin was immaculate. It even smelled good! The bonus was that I had already been paid for two additional nights that weren't used. *Winning!*

The advice we have if and when you should happen to observe your property being destroyed or abused is to chalk it up to wear-and-tear, budget for it, and try not to let it anger or upset you. Remember, you're a people person and since people will be people, this is what I mean by "you must forgive them their humanity." You can think of it as an opportunity for you, yourself to learn how to respect the property of others, and also teach your children the importance of this value. Meanwhile, pride yourself on your ability to fix things and then take it a step further:

I suggest you market your property as being "well-maintained."

As far as preparing yourself for the unexpected things people may say, just try not to let their words shock you. Be gracious when they compliment you and quiet when they insult you. Take responsibility when it is merited and always justify their complaints and their needs. It will cost you very little to be gracious. After all, most people truly only want one thing, and that's to know that they matter.

Many of your guests may come to matter a great deal to you. Week after week we have people stay with us who have become very good friends. Cleaning and preparing for them is like cleaning and preparing for family. We may only see each other once a year but we use that time to catch up and share stories, (we talk about our kids, a LOT), and we stay in touch after they leave Sandy Point. Making friends comes easily for me, so I'm not surprised that my job as an innkeeper has presented me with so many friendships. What I didn't expect is that these friends—and so many of our guests—would return year after year after year. I know they like me, but it's extremely rewarding to know how much they also like what we've created.

Having so many "super nice people and good friends" come into her life was also an unexpected bonus for one of my innkeeping colleagues, Loretta Zortman, owner of Mockingbird Bay Resort in Mountain Home, Arkansas. Loretta came into *my* life in an interesting way. I first met Loretta through a letter she wrote to me after reading *I'm Living Your Dream Life*. She and her husband, Frank, had been living in New York City and he worked on Wall Street during the terrorist attacks of September 11, 2001. "He survived the WTC attacks of September11th, but not the massive layoffs that followed," she wrote. According to Loretta, the story of our *Dream Life* encouraged them to pursue the business of innkeeping. Loretta wrote, "It was your book that turned the tables in my mind, and made me begin to consider the resort business as a lifestyle and family-run venture."

Well, they did more than consider it. They moved from New York to Arkansas in 2003 and took over the ownership of Mockingbird Bay Resort. Now here's the interesting part. The Zortmans purchased this resort from my friends, Tom and Judy Ligeikis, whom I had known most of my life. (Tom was the best man at my sister's wedding back in 1971). Tom had visited us at Sandy Point during our early years of operation and loved relating tips and stories about our shared occupations. And Judy was one of the first people to read and review my book. She, like many of the innkeepers I have heard from since its publication, definitely related to our story. Meanwhile, I was familiar with Mockingbird Bay Resort only though photos, and of course, Tom and Judy's stories from 15 years of ownership. I knew they had the resort on the market but could hardly believe the coincidence when they sold it to this woman who had written to me after reading my book!

Sadly, Tom passed away shortly after selling Mockingbird Bay Resort and I haven't stayed in touch with Judy to hear about life after innkeeping. I do correspond with Loretta, however, and enjoy hearing about life after Wall Street and how her experience is measuring up the dream life they had envisioned. I'm happy to report that she and Frank have survived eight years in the business and are going strong.

Loretta cited Mother Nature as continually handing them unexpected surprises. They didn't have anything as dramatic as their lake disappearing like the resort owners on Lake Delton in the spring of 2009; however, in the summer of 2011 she said their lake, Lake Norfork, rose 20 feet in three days. "We had to adjust the dock every two hours to keep up with the rising water."

Adjusting a dock or firing up a generator are relatively easy solutions to temporary situations handed to you by Mother Nature. But say She wages a bit more wrath and sends a storm your way, which is packed with hurricane force winds that cause some real damage. You simply must be prepared with a stocked emergency kit and a backup plan.

Your emergency kit should include several flashlights and extra batteries. For spare candles, have matches or wand lighters. Include things like duct tape, a 3-way can opener and a 14-in-1 pocket tool or Swiss Army knife. Also be sure to have an AM/FM radio (with battery or batteries) and a phone that doesn't require electricity. Another thing to consider is to have available spare sleeping quarters or living space. What happens if a guest unit is either destroyed or rendered uninhabitable by the storm?

One of the worst freak acts of nature we experienced at Sandy Point was a microburst, which hit us in July, 2008. A microburst is defined as "a small, very intense downdraft that descends to the ground resulting in a strong wind divergence."[4] Aside from the cerise red sky we woke up to on that Friday morning and the credence we often pay to the old saying, "red sky at night—sailor's delight; red sky in the morn—sailors be warned," we didn't read the code red to warn

---

[4] "Microburst" by Judy Hedding, About .com Guide; http://phoenix.about.com/cs/weather/g/microburst.htm

of impending 100 mph winds that would momentarily crash down upon us that night.

It was just before midnight. The power was out and I tried to let the sound of driving rain pelting our roof lull me to sleep. But it's difficult to rest during a storm, because we don't know what's coming that might require us to spring into action. I distinctly recall being on the edge of sleep, when suddenly my eyes popped open. It was because there had been an indistinguishable noise and a very odd momentary change in the atmosphere. The noise was like a *whoosh* and a crack at the same time, and it felt as though I'd been punched in the stomach. I didn't feel pain, but I was briefly breathless. It was as though all the air had been sucked out of the room. "What was *that*!?" I gasped.

My husband was not next to me, but moments later he came into the room, still dressed. He had not yet gone to bed. I asked him if he knew what happened, and wondered if I had been dreaming. "I don't know," he said. "We might have lost a tree. I think it might be close by." With that, he grabbed a rain jacket and a flashlight and headed out of the room. I followed him.

Halfway down the stairs from our bedroom, we heard a loud knock on our front door. It was the guests staying in Cabin #1, "Karibu," guests who at that point had been staying with us during the same week in July for 16 years. "Uh . . . Mike and Michele?" they said. "A tree fell on our cabin."

After an uncontrollable "oh shit" moment, they assured us they were all okay, and even though they couldn't see well due to the lack of light and driving rain, they didn't think the damage was significant.

They were right. The mature poplar measuring about 16-inches in diameter had snapped in two with the top half of the tree falling upon the front porch of this 72 year-old cabin. The impact caused minor roof and eave damage and inside, only a hanging light crashed and broke. So, the good news was the cabin was still inhabitable and the long-term guests weren't so freaked out by the experience that they needed another place to sleep for the night. If they had—and we have had guests who've panicked the moment they heard thunder or saw lightening—we have spare living quarters in the lower level of our house. There are five beds, a bathroom, full kitchen, eating and living areas, and even a big screen television with all the premium channels.

Provided we've got the generator going, anyone afraid of a storm can hunker down in our lower level, turn up the volume on the Weather Channel and track the radar.

The bad news about this storm, and we didn't truly see it all until daylight, was that the tree atop "Karibu" was only one of 14 uprooted or snapped trees at the lakefront. Another tree had come close to hitting cabin #2, "Hilltop," but ultimately missed. Our boathouse, however, was completely obliterated by two trees, a birch and another white pine, and one of our wooden chair swings bit the dust after the top part of an ancient white pine—perhaps one of the oldest the property—snapped off and fell upon it.

The whole scene was, in a word, odd. Two beautiful white pines that once flanked the fish-cleaning hut like sentries standing guard were both completely uprooted and laid flat to the ground as though they had been shot. Our docks were twisted and mangled, boats were overturned, and several had been transported over 100 feet into the woods off the shore. Our swim rafts and water trampoline were missing. The flagpoles were in the water, and the wooden jungle gym had disappeared into the forest. We knew we faced hours and hours of cleanup and repair.

Now, are you ready for the punch line? It was a Saturday. Of course, in addition to all the additional cleanup, we also faced a full turnover with new guests arriving at 4:00 p.m.

You may be curious as to how we got through it. First of all, we kept a good sense of humor. In fact, as the departing guests surveyed the damage and said their goodbyes, they couldn't understand why we were laughing. "What else can we do?" I responded. "It's either laugh or cry, or maybe lose my mind!" Some of the guests actually stuck around after the 9:00 a.m. checkout and helped us cleanup. Kids gathered sticks and branches, parents swept and raked and offered lots of neighborly moral support. We definitely needed help, and we called other neighbors to come by to remove the tree from cabin #1, "Karibu," and repair the roof and eave, while we preceded to turnover all the cabins for the afternoon check-in deadline.

We did make our deadline and the new guests staying in cabin #1, "Karibu" never knew what hit it. The docks and the damage to the beach and beach equipment took a while longer to get back into shape, but again, with help from some of our guests, we even managed to save a stand of uprooted birch trees by pulling them back into their place on the shore. Like us, to this day they're still surviving.

In order to be a successful innkeeper, the only way to truly be prepared is to learn to expect the unexpected. Be patient, gracious and kind. Have backup plans and equipment in place, and understand you may often be required to get creative, to think and act quickly, and to ask for help when necessary.

Chapter 8:
Cleaning Tips and Checklists

The first and most important opinions a guest forms about your establishment are based on how clean it is. Thanks to several recent media exposés, some seasoned travelers have come to expect unsanitary conditions in hotel and motel rooms—at both luxury hotels and roadside inns. I wonder who hasn't heard the recommendation that hotel bedspreads be removed at once and never used as a blanket? As a result of several studies, both scientific and anecdotal, germaphobes and alarmists have helped turn the antibacterial cleanser industry into a multi-billon dollar business. You will be contributing to this business.

As an innkeeper of a small resort or bed-and-breakfast, you are in a different category than a large hotel. And this is good news. Because you are more intimately involved with the cleaning of your property, you have greater control of its cleanliness. Remember, you ARE your establishment. And I suggest that you prepare every space as though your best friend or your child were staying there.

Cleaning styles vary and it's not my intention to tell you how you should specifically go about cleaning your cabins, cottages, condos or guestrooms or what products you should use. As I implied earlier, you are required to do a professional job, and approach the job in terms relating to not only cleanliness, but also "sanitization." I focus primarily on bathrooms, kitchens and bedrooms.

An innkeeper's role as housekeeper isn't only about changing beds and sweeping sandy floors. And to give credence to the so-called germaphobes, you must keep in mind that not all of your guests will be 100 percent healthy. According to a study conducted by the University of Virginia, people with colds leave contagious germs on nearly 35 percent of the objects they touch, and 80 percent of all infectious diseases are transmitted by contact. A virus may live for at least a day on objects such as doorknobs and faucet handles. It is therefore essential that the products you choose to clean your facilities contain antibacterial compounds.

Bathrooms

Did you know that over the course of a lifetime, the average person spends three years on a toilet? I believe as innkeepers, we owe it to our customers to make a trip to the toilet as nice an experience as possible. Keep in mind a toilet is a toilet is a toilet. Your job is to clean it well and try to get over the fact that you're doing it.

Occasionally when I'm cleaning a toilet I remember a scene from the 1982 film *Ghandi* starring Ben Kingsley as Mohandas Ghandi. The film portrays Ghandi's non-violent movement toward gaining equal rights for all Indian people in South Africa and his ensuing campaign to promote peace between religious groups (Muslim and Hindu) in India and Pakistan. In the film, Ghandi's wife, played by Rohini Hattangadi, is at first reluctant toward the drastic lifestyle change her husband's campaign requires. She, for example, is given the chore of cleaning the latrines. "It is the work of untouchables," she says. And to this her husband replies, "In this place there are no untouchables, and no work is beneath any of us." A dutiful wife, she succumbs to the chore.

In case you're unfamiliar with the term, in Hindu society, an "untouchable" is a person belonging to the lowest caste or social group. Do not think of your work cleaning toilets and bathrooms as lower class work. Instead, think about how pleased your guests will be when they find a fresh-smelling, germ-free room with sparkling porcelain and chrome. Don't forget to disinfect the toilet flusher and the underside of the seat, which are two of the most germ infested parts of any toilet.

Also, use a new rag for each area you clean: the toilet, the sink, the medicine cabinet, the shower/bath.

On your cleaning checklist, don't forget the toilet paper fold. We like to refer to the toilet paper fold as "toilet paper origami." A toilet paper fold tells the guests, in effect, that the room has been cleaned with care. We use the simple triangular fold because it's fast and easy, and it's a good way to make use of a roll that's not brand new, yet, of course, contains plenty of unused tissue.

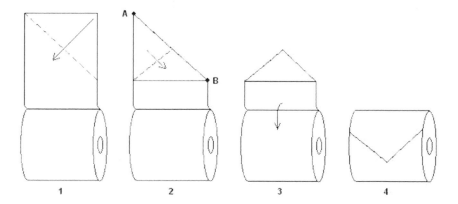

Triangular fold, step by step:[5]

1. Use either a full (new) roll or a roll currently on the dispenser. The tearing end should be over the top of the roll. Note: Paper should measure at least one-inch thick around the roll in order to provide enough squares for several uses prior to inconveniencing guests with the task of changing the roll. (Remove rolls with insufficient squares and add to your personal supply). Pull out two-to-three squares of paper and stretch it above the roll. Fold the top right corner down to form a right angle triangle.

2. Join point A to point B, folding down the top left corner to form an isosceles triangle.

3. Lay the triangular point back down, atop the roll, and press flat.

4. Triangular fold complete.

[5] Origami Research Center, http://www.origami-resource-center.com

There are fancier ways to fold toilet paper; and by all means, if you have the time and inclination experiment. The Origami Resource Center gives step-by-step instructions for the diamond fold, the pleated fold, and the pleated tuck. There are also books that depict a host of creative toilet paper folds, including sailboats, butterflies and flowers. Perhaps these experiments might be something to consider during your slow or off seasons, especially if you have an unfulfilled creative urge.

Procter & Gamble, the manufacturers of Charmin toilet tissue, reports that a standard roll of toilet paper lasts five days in the most-used bathroom of an average household. According to P&G's study, customers use 8.6 sheets per trip, or 57 sheets per day. Use these figures to determine the number of rolls you provide in each bathroom. Remember not to overstock, so as not to encourage guests to overuse the supply—especially if you have septic systems. On that note, the Charmin studies have further shown that ordinary toilet paper does not harm septic systems, so there's not an absolute need to buy bio-degradable or expensive tissues specially marketed for septic systems. Cheaper brands may, in fact, break down quicker and more completely than the softer, fluffier brands with perfumes and softeners, but by all means, don't use one-ply paper. That's just uncomfortable and frankly, not very classy.

Other types of papers, such as newspapers, facial tissue, and writing or document papers should never be flushed into a septic system. Reference the "Ode to the Septic Tank" poem in Chapter 5.

Okay, enough about toilet paper. By now the suggestion that toilets and yes, toilet tissue will play a large role in your life as an innkeeper is apparent. But there's something even more unpleasant about bathroom cleaning that I simply must warn you about, and that's how much you'll be dealing with human hair.

A couple facts about follicles: There are 100,000 to 150,000 hair follicles per head and the average person loses 50 to 200 strands of hair per day. And where are they predominantly losing it? In the bathrooms you are required to clean.

Losing hair is a perfectly natural process. Hair goes through a growth cycle—the growth phase (anagen, which accounts for 85-90 percent of the hair on your head), the transitional phase (catagen, affecting 5 percent) and the resting phase (telogen, 10 percent), which is the phase when most hairs are shed. The overall growth cycle of each follicle lasts six to eight years and follicles are constantly renewing themselves. Granted, some guests may be hairier than others, as the evidence left in your bathrooms may suggest, but trust, ridding bathrooms of human hairs is key to a successful cleaning. Even one hair left behind will mean your new inhabitants won't notice the pleasant aroma of cleaning supplies or the shine of the faucet. I promise you, if guests find a hair in the sink or bathtub—or anywhere in the unit—your credibility as a clean establishment will go down the toilet.

Finally, regarding the bathroom cleaning process, we have found that most guests tend to shower on the morning before they leave. This translates into wet shower curtains at turnover time. If you have glass doors, this isn't an issue; however, with glass doors you should supply a squeegee, and this is an item that has a short shelf life. Shower curtains, on the other hand, require special attention, and you must check for mildew with each turnover. Cleaning or preparing shower curtains can be time-consuming. We have tried a lot of different shower curtains over the years and have settled on a fabric "hookless" variety from a manufacturer called Arcs & Angles. The company markets it as a "10 second hookless shower curtain." Ten seconds refers to the amount of time it takes to either remove the curtain from or place it on the shower rod. Remember, when you're dealing with multiple bathrooms, time is of the essence. The curtains are made of durable polyester fabric and are machine washable. They don't need to be laundered every week; however, when they're wet from a recent shower and it's a nice day, it's a quick and easy chore to slip the hookless variety off the rod and hang it to dry on an outdoor clothesline. Just remember on your final inspection, to check whether or not the curtains have been taken off the clothesline and hung back in place.

Bathroom Turnover Checklist
Supplies
- ☐ Toilet bowl brush
- ☐ Toilet bowl cleaner
- ☐ Bathroom disinfectant/anti-bacterial cleaner
- ☐ Glass cleaner (for bathroom mirror)
- ☐ 6-10 clean rags

☐ Scrubber sponge
☐ Toilet paper supply
☐ Handi-vac/broom
☐ Floor mop/cleaner
☐ Bathroom rug
☐ Wastebasket liner

Cleaning
☐ Toilet bowl
☐ Toilet seat (upside/underside)
☐ Toilet flusher handle
☐ Toilet base
☐ Bathtub/shower walls and floor
☐ Bathtub/shower faucet and handles
☐ Shower curtain
☐ Sink basin
☐ Sink faucet and handles
☐ Backsplash area
☐ Medicine cabinet shelves
☐ Mirror
☐ Replenish toilet paper supply
☐ Replace wastebasket liner
☐ Toilet paper fold
☐ Sweep/vacuum/mop floor
☐ Replace floor rug or bath mat

Kitchens

Cleaning kitchens is my job. I can pawn off the bathrooms and bedrooms, but our staff leaves the kitchens to me. It's not because of the appliances and the heavy-duty cleaning that is sometimes required for ovens, stovetops and refrigerators. It's because of the utensils.

Since kitchen utensils have a constant turnover, it takes a keen eye, a strong ability to be thorough and an adequate backup supply. We, for example, no longer offer a full set of matching flatware in any of our cabins. But a set of forks that are 100 percent the same isn't what's important. In fact, more than once I've heard guests say that our mismatched flatware only adds to the charm of the cabin. What is important about the flatware is making sure we have a certain number of each piece in each unit. For example, we supply eight forks, knives and spoons in each two-bedroom unit, ten of each in the three-bedroom units and sixteen in our four-bedroom unit. Since we have to sterilize the flatware between uses, it's very easy to count pieces in the process. It is a rare week when I don't have to replace a piece of flatware.

I have a theory as to why spoons often go missing and it's based on how my own kids often grab them for ice cream, yogurt and fruit cups and transport them away from kitchens and dining tables. Even though I don't often find spoons around the grounds of Sandy Point, I surmise this is what guests do as well and guess further that they accidently toss the spoons in the trash with the empty containers of yogurt and fruit. Forks and knives, on the other hand, are not as big a mystery. Groups renting more than one cabin tend to travel from cabin to cabin and take turns hosting nightly dinners. When guests have more than ten mouths to feed in one of our three bedroom units, the dinner invitation includes a BYOF (Bring Your Own Fork) proviso. Baking dishes, salad and serving bowls and glassware travel between cabins as well. So, in addition to cleaning each kitchen, every drawer, cabinet, cupboard and pantry must be checked and possibly restocked. I have labels on the cabinet doors asking guests to please return any pots and pans loaned from another cabin, but it doesn't always happen. I understand that I can't expect our guests to know every detail about what does and doesn't belong in their kitchen cupboards at the end of a week. So, I'm prepared to hunt for missing items stored in other cabins prior to making a trip to the extra supply storage area.

The first thing we do upon entering a cabin for turnover is open the windows to air out the odors. Next we go to the breaker box. There we turn off power to the refrigerator. It's far easier than heaving this sizable appliance from the wall and pulling the plug. In the early days of our ownership, none of our refrigerators were self-defrosting. So, part of the cleaning and turnover process required several hours for the layer of ice and frost to melt from the freezer walls. If your kitchens have old refrigerators, I suggest you invest in new

ones. Guests have come to expect all the comforts of home while on
vacation and that includes a full-size, frost-free freezer on their refrigerator. In rural areas operating on well pumps, automatic icemakers
aren't as practical; however, so if your refrigerators don't have them,
include ice trays. And since every hotel and motel in the world offers
free ice from an ice machine "down the hall," guests expect ice to be
readily available. We don't have an ice machine on property, nor do
we sell ice in our shop, although it is something we have considered.
Meantime, nearly every week guests leave behind bags of it, so we
store the abandoned bags in our spare freezer and when we have it
available, will supply immediate ice to any guest who asks for it. State
health codes have explicit regulations regarding storage and distribution of ice, so be sure to check these policies.

Even though our refrigerators no longer need time to defrost, I
still don't want to stick my head in a cold freezer in order to clean
it. This is why we continue to turn off power to the refrigerators on
turnover day. This also means that whatever perishables have been
left behind must be immediately transported to one of our spare refrigerators. Guests regularly leave frozen items such as popsicles and
ice cream, and condiments such as ketchup and mayonnaise. We call
all food left behind, "cabin booty," and it's a rare summer that we have
to buy our own ketchup.

Generally, I return power to the refrigerators during the cabin's
final inspection and hope there's enough time for the temperature to
be cold enough by check-in time. This, by the way, often comes up
when guests arrive early—particularly guests who are eager to get ice
cream into the freezer. "I'm sorry but the refrigerator in your cabin
isn't turned on just yet," I say. They often find this puzzling until I explain that I had to turn it off for cleaning purposes. It's ironic, because
guests—even those who arrive early—expect a clean cabin; but it may
not occur to them that it's a time-consuming and laborious process
that actually dictates the check-in time.

Without question, the most time-consuming chore when cleaning
a kitchen is the stove and oven. We offer gas (propane) stoves with
removable burner grates and drip bowls. For these parts, black finish
is better than gray or chrome, because black better hides the tough,
baked on stains. I deem it necessary to make the stoves look brand
new each week and unfortunately, most of our stoves have gray-
colored grates. Depending on how much stovetop cooking was done,

the gray grates can sometimes take 30 minutes to clean. The longer a stain has time to bake onto the appliance, the more difficult it is to remove. For this chore, I use bleach spray and a heavy-duty scouring pad, and my cleaning tray always includes at least three fresh pads.

When putting all this elbow grease into making our stovetops shine, I sometimes wonder if the incoming guests will even notice how clean it is. But each time, I dismiss this thought because I'm certain that they would notice if it were stained.

Guests don't tend to do a lot of heavy-duty baking while on vacation, so ovens don't merit a full cleaning each week. Granted, occasionally you'll need to deal with a pot roast or a turkey, or a prepared meal that requires extra time with your head in the oven, so have the oven cleaner product in your cleaning cart. Frozen pizzas, on the other hand, are a common quickie vacation option, and often they're placed directly on oven racks. Cheese will more often than not drip onto the oven surface. Our solution to this cleaning issue is to supply each oven with a removable aluminum liner. If you purchase liners in bulk, they cost less than $2.00 each, and are well worth the price for the amount of cleaning time they save.

The following is an extensive checklist for a fully stocked kitchen in a rental unit. It isn't necessary to supply everything listed here; however, it's meant to be a list of items for you to consider. We, for example, don't offer dishwashers in any of our units due primarily to the septic systems and kitchen space allowances. And only one of our units, the largest (Lakeview Lodge) offers a private laundry (washer and dryer) facility. Both the dishwasher and the additional washer/dryer units we once provided in the individual cabins proved to be detriments rather than assets due to overuse and flooding. Your dishwasher and washer/dryer at home may not regularly flood and cause wood floor or carpet damage, but our experience with those in our rental units did so regularly. All our guests must therefore wash their dishes by hand, and our centrally located laundry house, built in 2009, has proved to be a useful and appreciated guest amenity. We offer coin-operated devices and sell detergent and fabric softeners in our shop. Note this is not yet an income expansion success story. Given our investment in building the facility, which included installing a new septic system exclusive to the building, plus the cost of the coin-op washer and dryer, based on the quarters we've collected each season we may see a return on the investment in 62 years!

Large Appliances
- ☐ Full-size refrigerator with auto-defrost freezer (include ice cube trays)
- ☐ Oven with stovetop burners
- ☐ Dishwasher
- ☐ Washer and dryer

Small Appliances
- ☐ Coffee maker/pot
- ☐ Blender
- ☐ Microwave oven
- ☐ Toaster or toaster oven

Dinnerware
- ☐ Dinner plates
- ☐ Salad plates
- ☐ Cereal/soup bowls
- ☐ Flatware (forks, spoons, soup spoons, butter knives)*
- ☐ Steak knives
- ☐ Water/drinking glasses
- ☐ Coffee cups
- ☐ (Sturdy) Wine glasses
- ☐ A large serving platter

Baking/Cooking Accessories
- ☐ 9 x 13 Pyrex baking dish
- ☐ 8 x 8 Pyrex baking dish
- ☐ Cookie sheets/muffin tins
- ☐ Bread pan
- ☐ Large casserole dish
- ☐ Measuring spoons/measuring cups
- ☐ Sauce pans with lids, 1-1/2 to 4 quarts
- ☐ Large, 8-10-quart boiling pot with lid
- ☐ Frying pans
- ☐ Cast iron frying pan (for fish fry)
- ☐ Pizza pan
- ☐ Sharp paring/carving knives
- ☐ Potato/vegetable peeler
- ☐ Rubber spatula

- [ ] Colander
- [ ] Microwaveable dishes
- [ ] Soup ladle
- [ ] Tongs
- [ ] Serving spoons and wooden spoons
- [ ] Salad bowl
- [ ] Mixing bowls
- [ ] Cake pans
- [ ] Roaster with lid
- [ ] Slotted spoon/basting spoon
- [ ] Rolling pin
- [ ] Pie pan

Other
- [ ] Cutting board(s)
- [ ] Can/bottle opener
- [ ] Corkscrew
- [ ] Plastic pitcher
- [ ] Tea kettle/teapot
- [ ] Hot pads/trivets
- [ ] Fire extinguisher (required by the State)
- [ ] Ice cream scoop
- [ ] Pizza cutter
- [ ] Pot holders
- [ ] Kitchen scissors
- [ ] Matches or wand lighter
- [ ] Lined trash bin

Pantry Items
- [ ] Salt and pepper
- [ ] Coffee filters
- [ ] Sugar or sweetener
- [ ] Toothpicks

* Flatware supplies: Two-bedroom units, eight each; Three-bedroom units, 10 each; Four bedroom unit, 16 each. (Numbers based on established occupancy levels).

Bedrooms

The request we had most often in our early years was for more hooks in the bedrooms. Guests like to hang robes, towels and sweatshirts, and closet space in units is sometimes limited. Alarm clocks and good reading lights are also a nice touch. Each bedroom also needs a mirror. Many times guests are sharing cabins with friends or in-laws, and if the bathroom is down the hall rather than in the room, they want to check themselves first thing in the morning before bumping into someone or joining the group for coffee.

If you have ceiling fans in your bedrooms, dust them as a first chore, before you makeup the bed or beds. One should always dust a room from top to bottom, and for some reason, dust tends to collect on ceiling blade fans and slatted blinds faster than anywhere else.

After wiping down all the surfaces—dressers and nightstands, and if your bedrooms have televisions don't forget to disinfect the remote control—it's fastest and easiest and more fun to have two-persons making up each bed. Of course, clean sheets are always applied, but the mattress pad is not changed out each time between guests. It is essential that bed-makers examine the pads for stains and apply a new, clean pad from storage, if needed. It's very difficult to treat blood and urine stains and launder in time to meet your turnover deadline. You are not required to wash blankets, quilts and bedspreads between every new guest, but you must maintain a regular washing cycle and certainly check for stains or other damages. Be prepared to replace these items when necessary.

Additional tip: Don't forget to look under the beds. If a guest finds a sock or bathing suit top under the bed, it will have a similar affect as finding a hair in the bathtub or a stain on the stovetop grate. Guests may assume you weren't paying close attention to the overall cleaning process.

Don't be surprised by the items your guests leave behind, and note, most of these items are left in the bedrooms. Nearly every week someone forgets to pack a phone charger. They are most often found on nightstands or plugged into sockets near them. Kid's toys are high on the list, followed by clothing items. Once someone left the contents of an entire suitcase in one of the dressers, and unfortunately, we didn't check the drawers in that bedroom on that turnover day. We didn't know the clothes had been forgotten until after the next guests left and they informed us through a letter indicating how offensive it was to have found the clothes of a previous guest. We never heard from the owner of the clothes, so we ultimately weren't sure who had left them.

Our policy about returning items is informal. In most cases, we wait to hear from the guest about what items are missing because sometimes it's difficult to keep track of the things we find in the cabins, on the grounds or in the outbuildings. More valuable items like iPods, for example, or a pair of men's ostrich skin cowboy boots, which I once found in a bedroom closet, make a greater impression and we let guests know we've found their possessions as soon as possible. The boots were heavy, so I sent them C.O.D.; however, the many iPods and phone chargers I've returned over the years have been at our expense. In most instances, grateful guests have sent a thank-you note along with a check for five bucks to cover the postage. For the record, a guest has never asked to have us return a stray sock, pajama piece or any kind of undergarment. In addition to many Teddy bears or other precious toys of toddlers, we have also returned too many cosmetic bags and dopp kits to count.

We dress our beds with quilts and bed skirts, and both items tend to tear at the seams. I repair them with dental floss, a sturdy thread. Sometimes guests are tempted to use bed quilts as picnic tablecloths or beach blankets. If you don't want this to happen, post a sign reading "Quilts, blankets and throws are for indoor use only." We store extra pillows, blankets and pillowcases in bedroom closets, along with spare sheets for the convertible sofas or futons. It doesn't happen often, but occasionally pillows go missing. Many guests bring their own bed pillows along to supplement our supply and I think they may sometimes confuse which pillows belong to them and which belong to the Resort. Don't forget to check the supply and have spares as backup.

Bedroom Cleaning Checklist
- ☐ collect soiled sheets
- ☐ inspect mattress pads/blankets/quilts
- ☐ ceiling fan
- ☐ windowsills and curtains
- ☐ wipe down/disinfect all furniture surfaces

- [ ] television remote control
- [ ] alarm clock
- [ ] check dresser drawers
- [ ] check underneath bed
- [ ] check closet/hanger supply
- [ ] check supply of spare blankets/pillows/pillowcases
- [ ] makeup bed (use hospital corners)
- [ ] vacuum or mop floor

Miscellaneous Tips

Odors: Many mornings while I'm out for a run and ultimately come within smelling distance of the cabins, the unmistakable aroma of frying pork products fills my olfactory sense. This was one of the first things we learned about guests on vacation—at least guests in the Northwoods. They like a big breakfast. Also, depending on how the fish are biting during the week, they love a traditional Friday night fish fry.

Lingering cooking odors are the biggest challenge when it comes to making cabins or units smell fresh. You can burn scented candles or spray the room with air freshener; however, these techniques tend to mask the odors rather than rid them from the atmosphere.

Cleaning the stove and oven is the first step and next we double-check the cookware for any remaining evidence of the prepared food. A tip from *Good Housekeeping* to zap kitchen odors is to mix three tablespoons of white vinegar and one cup of water and boil in a small saucepan for several minutes. (Vinegar is acidic and odors are alkaline, so the former neutralizes the latter).

Our units are all designated "non-smoking," but that doesn't mean every guest complies. In fact, I think there's been quite a backlash by smokers due to all of the recent regulations against smoking in any enclosed place. On July 5, 2010, Wisconsin joined 32 other states that prohibited smoking in public places whether privately or publicly owned. This includes workplaces, restaurants and taverns. Smokers may believe that because they are paying to rent your facilities that they should be allowed to smoke there, regardless of the law. The clean indoor air law allows for a $10 fine for illegal smoking. Further, the state of Wisconsin's Department of Health and Family Services provides printed cards regarding an act warning guests of penalties for careless smoking habits. It's Act 254.76 "Stats. Causing Fires by Tobacco Smoking. (1) Any person who, by smoking, or attempting to light or to smoke cigarettes, cigars, pipes or tobacco, in any manner in which lighters or matches are employed, shall, in a careless, reckless or negligent manner, set fire to any bedding, furniture, curtains, drapes house or any household fittings, or any part of any building specified in sub. (2), so as to endanger life or property in any way or to any extent, shall be fined not less than $50 nor more than $250, together with costs, or imprisoned not less than 10 days nor more than 6 months or both." Part (2) of the notice indicates that a printed notice shall be kept posted in a "conspicuous place advising tenants of the provisions of this section."

To give smokers a place to smoke, we request "as a courtesy to the guests who follow," that smokers use the screen porches for smoking, and supply ashtrays there. Even when guests do use the porch, however, occasionally the smoke odors travel into the cabin. We can tell the moment we walk into any cabin whether or not cigarettes, cigars or pipes have been smoked. The challenge is to make it so that the next guests don't have the same experience. The same methods we use for ridding the cabin of cooking odors tend to work for smoke odors, but occasionally we find it necessary to use a product designated specifically for smoke odors. We use Smoke Odor Eliminator by National Interchem Corp. Back in the 1960s, when you couldn't host a neighborhood coffee klatch, cocktail or Tupperware party without smokers infiltrating your home, I remember my mother set out tiny bowls of vanilla extract as a combative measure. Knowing her, this was a Hint from Heloise, and it works. Plus, vanilla is a homier aroma than vinegar. To remove cigarette smoke odors from fabrics—such as pillows and upholstery—sprinkle baking soda, leave it there for a couple hours and then vacuum.

Vacuums: A vacuum is a high-maintenance but necessary appliance. One should be supplied in each housekeeping unit. I think we've tried nearly every brand of vacuum on the market, and no matter how much we spend on any given vacuum, they all are in need of constant attention. If your vacuums use bags, have a large supply on hand. And don't forget to check the bags for replacement with each turnover. Whenever possible, change vacuum bags or empty dirt containers outdoors. If your vacuum doesn't seem to be suctioning properly or picking up the dirt, chances are the beater bar is tied up. It's most likely because of that culprit human hair. Try to keep up with hair removal with weekly maintenance, before freeing the beater bar becomes an extremely time-consuming project.

Fireplaces: In cooler climates or for romantic weekend getaways, indoor fireplaces are a highly marketable amenity. Along with fireplaces, however, come added liability and maintenance. First of all, fireplaces will be inspected for safety and may affect your insurance rates. You must also either supply firewood or make it available. Fireplaces may also be a nuisance to clean. It is both messy and time consuming to shovel and dispose of ashes. We provide a set of fireplace tools as well as a metal bucket on the hearths of our fireplaces and ask guests via a sign on the mantle to do us the favor of cleaning it prior to departure. Thankfully, not many choose to burn fires indoors during the busy summer months, as they opt for outdoor campfires instead. During the summer months, however, we keep fireplace dampers open, just to avoid the occasional calamity of a guest starting a fire and filling the room with smoke. It happens. With multiple smoke alarms required in each unit, be assured they'll all scream with ear-splitting urgency in the event of a smoke-filled room. Smoke alarms are extremely sensitive and can go off in the event a cook lets the bacon fry a bit too long. We sometimes find one or more smoke alarms dismantled with a nine-volt battery either missing or dangling from the unit. Adding a check on the smoke alarms is something to add to your final inspections each week. It's also worth noting that smoke odors from outdoor fire pits can also penetrate into the cabin—particularly on windy days. This is a caution for placing or constructing outdoor fire pits well away from windows.

Bats, Bed Bugs and other Bothersome Pests: It's been a long time since we've heard the blood-curdling scream of a guest who has encountered a bat in his cabin. Before we tore down the original cabins, bats were regular visitors. And no matter how hard we may have tried to dispel the myth that bats are biting vampires or hair-nesters, or tout the fact that bats help keep the mosquito population down, it was little comfort to the terrified guest.

Bats are hosts for diseases such as rabies, however, only one half of one percent of all bats tested have been found to carry rabies. Nevertheless, all contact should be avoided.

The bat eradication process has undergone quite an evolution over the past 20 years and I think we've used every method known to man, including the extreme method of actually tearing down an infested cabin. The problem with bats is that while they may appear to be large in flight, they're actually very small and will work their way through an opening as small as half an inch. This is the size of a human thumb. The latest and most humane method of bat eradication is to first identify the entry point. One way to do this is to observe the suspected areas (eaves and fireplace flues, for example) at dawn, when bats return "home" after a long night of feeding. Next, a one-way mesh is applied so that the bats can get out but they can't get back inside. Once they're out, caulk the holes. This process should be done in spring or autumn rather than the summer when babies are present. Baby bats can't fly and will therefore starve to death once their parents/food sources are shut out.

Bats will need someplace to go once you seal them out. Rather than risk having them find the smallest openings of one of your other guest units or public places, install a bat house nearby the freshly abandoned dwelling. Hang the bat house on the southwest side of a building rather than a tree. It should be placed 15-20 feet off the ground and, if possible, within a quarter mile of a body of water.

Bed bugs were thought to be eradicated in the United States decades ago and we hadn't heard anything about them until a couple years ago when reports of a bed bug resurgence caught media attention. Initially the reports focused on big city hotels—even luxury hotels. The resurgence was attributed to international travelers carrying infested luggage. Unfortunately, people don't always spot bugs on their baggage before traveling to their next destination. The bugs get into beds because often, the first place a guest places his bag on the bed.

Bed bugs are tiny, tick-like creatures, and they can be seen with the naked eye. If one of your mattresses has them, you will see them—or at least see evidence of them. All you need to do is look. If a mattress has bed bugs, you will most likely see reddish brown excrement spots or evidence of dander or shells before finding the bugs themselves. They like to burrow into the crevices. Don't wait for your guests to report what they believe to be bed bug bites. Check your mattresses as part of the bed-making process.

You might not always hear about bed bug bites as they don't appear immediately. Bed bug bites usually take a week to nine days to show up. They look like small mosquito bites or like the bites of sand fleas or chiggers. The small red welts often present in sets of three, as according to experts, "bed bugs like to eat breakfast, lunch and dinner." The bites are itchy but not dangerous, and these bugs don't transmit diseases. Some people, however, may have an allergic reaction. If they're scratched too much, bites can get infected.

Should your property experience a bed bug infestation, bear in mind it's not because your facilities aren't clean. Bed bugs are equal opportunity infesters and there's not much you can do to prevent them. Except for one major cautionary: Never ever purchase a used mattress. In some states selling used mattresses is illegal. To find out what the bedding laws are in your state, contact the State Departments of Health, Consumer Affairs, Agriculture or Licensing. Meanwhile, you can remedy the situation and help prevent your guests from becoming bed bug victims. Thoroughly inspect any mattress you may suspect, or call your regular exterminator to check it for bed bug evidence. If evidence is found, I suggest you dispose the mattress and fumigate the bedroom. One way to assure your disposed mattress won't be pilfered from the dump or reused in any capacity is to make multiple slits in it to destroy its functionality.

In my book *I'm Living Your Dream Life: The Story of a Northwoods Resort Owner*, I wrote about what we call the "bug de jour" factor when referring to the host of bothersome, biting flies in our neck of the woods. The consistent and predictable bugs are the spring black flies or gnats, which only last for a few days in May. They are followed by the mosquitoes, which peak at the 4th of July and then, depending on rainfall levels, diminish through the remaining summer months. In the warmest part of the summer the peskiest of pesky, the deerflies, take up residence.

Bugs are not your fault but when it comes to guest comfort, they are your concern. For mosquitoes, we recommend anything with DEET, such as Deep Woods Off or Repel. For deerflies, I'm afraid there isn't a product we know that repels them or keeps them from circling your head while you're hiking. A tip we offer, however, is to raise your arm above your head. These flies tend to circle around the highest point, and at least that takes the focus off your head. Another approach is to place a piece of double-stick tape on the back of your cap. It attracts deerflies like proverbial flypaper and again, keeps them from swarming around your head. Just remember to remove your cap and remove the tape and inevitable dead flies because it's not a pretty sight.

Maintenance Equipment Checklist

Whether your grounds are extensive or modest, they are responsible for presenting guests (and potential guests) with a first impression when arriving at your property. Mowed lawns, trimmed trees, planted flowers and swept walkways make for a welcoming environment. In real estate terms it's referred to as "curb appeal."

The following list contains items that are both absolute necessities (Standard tool kit and plumber's snake, for example) and others that are either optional or climate based like a skid-steer or a snowplow. We invested in a Bobcat skid-steer in the year 2000, which was a $22,000 expense. It was especially valuable in assisting with the construction of the disc golf course, and it also comes in handy for clearing large fallen trees after storms. With the excavating bucket attachment, this large machine is what we now use each spring to clear the beach from the inevitable mountain of sticks, leaves and debris that gather on our shoreline after the ice breaks. It turns days of work into hours.

If some of the items on this list seem frivolous or excessive to you, consider we've been doing this for 20 years and all of this equipment has proved useful and necessary. For instance, we use the power planer several times per summer to repair or adjust wooden doors that expand and warp as a means of normal wear and tear. Sometimes, depending on the humidity, doors can warp overnight. One guest will be fine with the state of the bathroom door on Friday, but the new guest on Saturday will come to you in disbelief that you offer a bathroom door that won't fully close.

As much as you try to provide your guests with "perfect" accommodations, as anyone who owns a home can tell you, they are a source of endless maintenance. It's important to communicate to your guests that if they discover any problems, or if anything is malfunctioning, they should report it as soon as possible so you may rectify the situation. The following is included in the language of our cancellation policy on each reservation confirmation: "If something malfunctions in your cabin, we ask that you give us the opportunity to repair or rectify the situation as soon as reasonably possible." The keyword here is "reasonable," and with the right tools available, you can most likely assure your guests speedy solutions.

As an innkeeper your tools will be your best friends. Take good care of them with regular maintenance, and be sure to keep them well organized so that you can always find what you need in quick time.

- ☐ Air compressor
- ☐ Axe
- ☐ Battery charger
- ☐ Bench grinder (sharpening wheel)
- ☐ Bow saw
- ☐ Bobcat (skid-steer)
- ☐ Bungee cords
- ☐ Chainsaw
- ☐ Circular saw
- ☐ Digging spade
- ☐ Drill
- ☐ Dump cart
- ☐ Extended pole pruner chainsaw
- ☐ Flashlights
- ☐ Garden spade and square-head shovel
- ☐ Generator(s)
- ☐ Golf or utility cart
- ☐ Hand spade
- ☐ Hatchet
- ☐ Hose/ spray nozzle
- ☐ Jumper cables
- ☐ Lawn sprinkler

- ☐ Leaf blower
- ☐ Loppers
- ☐ Miter saw
- ☐ Plastic rakes
- ☐ Plumbing snake/toilet auger
- ☐ Posthole digger
- ☐ Power auger
- ☐ Power planer
- ☐ Push lawnmower
- ☐ Push broom
- ☐ Pressure washer
- ☐ Ratchet Set
- ☐ Recycling storage containers
- ☐ Riding lawnmower
- ☐ Ropes
- ☐ Saw horses
- ☐ Sawzall
- ☐ Snowplow
- ☐ Snow shovels
- ☐ Seed spreader
- ☐ Standard tool kit
- ☐ Tarps
- ☐ Utility knife/blades
- ☐ Voltmeter
- ☐ Wire cutters
    (contained in most standard tool kits, but used A LOT)
- ☐ Wheelbarrow
- ☐ Wire rakes
- ☐ Wire ties
- ☐ X-acto knife/blades

Chapter 9:
Does Real Life Imitate the Dream?

We lived in Oakland, California when we bought Sandy Point Resort. High atop the east bay hills in a neighborhood called Montclair, our 1,300 square-foot starter home was surrounded by tall pines and eucalyptus trees, and we had a view of San Francisco Bay. For a newly married couple, owning a home in this desirable neighborhood—fixing it up, planting a garden—it felt like a dream life.

We didn't know it at the time, but the projects we undertook at our first house turned out to be our training ground for becoming innkeepers. Completely remodeling and decorating this two-bedroom, one-bath home, we tore out built-in room dividers that initially made the place look like a doctor's office. We then replaced all the flooring with hardwoods, terra cotta and enamel tile. We painted every room, including the bricks of the fireplace, and we stenciled the closet doors with original designs. We installed all new fixtures in the kitchen and bathroom, added French doors to the patio and hung new curtains on the enormous picture windows. Ripping out an abundance of weeds and overgrowth, we unearthed scores of beautiful rhododendrons, and other exotics like holly, jasmine and Japanese maple trees. After planting hundreds of iris, lily and tulip bulbs and countless hours of work and watering, passing neighbors out walking their dogs regularly rewarded our efforts with high praise.

I was a newspaper columnist at the time and one of my favorite pieces was entitled, "My Foggy Garden." (This work is reprinted in my second book, *The Things I Wish I'd Said*). The piece was more than an ode to my garden. In it I examined what the act of gardening had taught me about myself, including my propensity to obsess over helping things "grow and thrive with constant care and attention." Read: more training for my future in business as an innkeeper. It also made me recognize my affinity for "home."

"The fog covers this Montclair hillside like a blanket pulled up tightly when the sun drops behind the tallest trees and the furthest mountain range, and it lasts through the morning. It closes us off, protects us from the rest of the world. It makes me never want to leave home." [6]

Yes indeed, while living in the Oakland hills during the dreamy, romantic early years of our marriage, to me it was like heaven. But, of course, we didn't live in heaven, nor were we in a dream. The mortgage was steep and property taxes were high. We had to work many hours per week, Mike on the trading floor in downtown San Francisco and I at the community newspaper office in downtown Montclair. And because we lived in the forest—albeit an urban forest—deer came around daily and fed on the flowers I'd planted and cultivated. Then in 1991, an enormous fire known as "the Oakland Hills Firestorm" wiped out the homes of many of our neighbors, including colleagues with whom I worked. Although we were evacuated on that fateful October night, the fire stopped within one mile of our home and our property was spared.

We didn't move away from California because of the fire nor did we leave because of the earthquake that devastated the area two years prior. We weren't running away from our life. In spite of waking up to the relatively harsh reality of the hard work it took to meet the costs of maintaining the lifestyle we had chosen, we remained optimistic regarding our prospects. We believed there was something more— something we could do together that would be far more fulfilling. So, we moved in the direction we thought would help us achieve a vision we had created for our future.

I explain how we initially developed the idea of becoming innkeepers in *I'm Living Your Dream Life*, which in part involved an ex-

---

[6] *The Things I Wish I'd Said*, Michele VanOrt Cozzens. McKenna Publishing Group, Indian Wells, CA. 2004.

tended trip I took to Kenya, East Africa to visit my sister, Gayle, who lived there at the time. My sister and I stayed at several different guest ranches, camps and resorts across the country. One in particular, a family-owned and operated ranch called Lewa Downs in Laikipia, had an enormous impact on helping me formulate what would become our vision. Owned by the Craig family, second-generation son, William and his wife, Emma, offered charming guest facilities, stone huts with thatched roofs. They served meals on the garden veranda of their home, which we ate with them and their young daughters. The Craig's cattle ranching operation started in the early 1920s, when they acquired the 45,000-acre property at the base of Mt. Kenya, and continued to thrive. Also on property at Lewa Downs were a weaving mill/rug-making operation and a fledgling rhino sanctuary, (now world-renowned), which was developed by a woman named Anna Merz. During our brief stay at Lewa, I observed this young couple, William and Emma Craig, effectively combining their passions and family life with their business, and I was especially impressed by the way they exposed their children to an education offered by series of world travelers coming and going. I have recently learned that Lewa is where Prince William and Kate Middleton were staying when the Prince proposed marriage. World travelers, indeed!

Mike and I didn't have children at the time we first considered the innkeeping business, but hoped and believed they'd be a part of our future. We feel forever blessed to have given birth to our beautiful, healthy daughters, Willow and Camille. Of course, we didn't realize until we had kids how much they would change our lives. Yet we soon realized that children would have changed life as we knew it no matter what our occupation/s. As self-employed innkeepers, the good news is that we could always have them near us; but that was the bad news as well. Before our children were old enough to help run the resort, naturally they required constant attention and often—on Saturdays for example—on-site childcare. I'm not sure there's a job outside of nanny or childcare worker that anyone can do truly well with a baby on her hip. Meanwhile, in the innkeeping business, the property needs constant attention—seven days per week and 24 hours per day—and often, it feels as though the guests need something similar to childcare!

As an ironic result, parenting became more unexpected training for the job of innkeeping.

The more important point to consider is that the innkeeping business has definitely afforded our children an outstanding, memorable and happy childhood. They've been trained in many valuable aspects of running the business and have experienced all the benefits of what this vacation destination has to offer. I can say with complete certainty that our girls have developed a passion for all things "Wisconsin." As they spend only summers there—away from GPAs and AP courses, friends and frenemies, coaches and teachers, and high school highs along with high school drama—it is their Mecca. We won't require them to takeover the business when they are capable, but they will have that option. Sandy Point Resort is our legacy to our children and theirs' to inherit—God willing.

Our passion for parenting may have come after we developed our initial business plan; however, what we did have a passion for prior to the arrival of our children and our acquisition of Sandy Point Resort was the sport of disc golf. In the early years of our marriage we played golf daily after work and spent most of our weekends traveling to tournaments around the state of California. Mike, who had been playing disc golf since he was 14 years old, wanted his future to include the game. And because I intended to be a permanent part of Mike's future, I not only took up the sport, I also joined the PDGA (Professional Disc Golf Association), competed in tournaments, designed artwork for golf discs and learned how to become a tournament director.

Disc golf as an organized sport began with a man named Ed Headrick, known to all in the Frisbee community as "Steady Ed." He is credited with the invention of the modern day Frisbee while working for Wham-O Toys in the 1960s. Headrick designed the first official target or "hole," for the game he based on traditional golf (known in disc golf circles as "ball golf" or "stick golf"). His disc catching device, a "disc pole hole," is a basket made of galvanized steel and chain links (US Patent 4,039,189, issued in 1975).

Steady Ed had a vision for advancing disc sports and in addition to his inventions, he founded the Professional Disc Golf Association, the International Frisbee Association, the Recreational Disc Golf Association, the Junior Frisbee Championship and the World Frisbee Championship. Ed was a dear friend. We knew him well, played golf with him many times in California and he visited us in Wisconsin shortly after our daughter, Willow, was born in 1995. It was at Sandy

Point, which he dubbed "a disc golf sanctuary," that he formulated the Recreational Disc Golf Association. The last time I spoke with him was in August of 2002 when he was in a Florida hospital room. He died a few days later.

My husband is not an inventor like our friend, Ed, and is not as revered or as well-known. (Ed, for example, even appeared with Johnny Carson on the *Tonight Show* in 1966). Mike, however, inspired by Ed and other Frisbee legends such as Victor Malafronte, Stancil Johnson and Dan "Stork" Roddick—to name a few—also had a vision that involved disc golf.

In the early 1980s, Mike saw that he could supply his personal golf disc equipment a lot more economically if he bought discs in bulk at a wholesale rate, take his stash, and then sell the remainders to fellow golfers. The course he and his buddies played regularly, Aquatic Park in Berkeley, California, sits beside an estuary of San Francisco Bay. The holes, particularly on the front nine of 18, present water hazards that teach any beginning golfer not to become emotionally attached to his or her discs. One attractive aspect of disc golf vs. ball golf is that the equipment is far less expensive. But that isn't the case when one risks throwing a driver into a saltwater estuary on the first hole of every round. Discs weighing 175 to 180 grams sink right to the swampy bottom!

Mike enlisted the help of a friend on the Trading Floor and designed his first disc "hot stamp," the now classic "Berkeley Aquatic Park" stamp, and placed a custom order of what became highly desirable discs. Hence, his business as an Innova golf disc dealer began. Today, not only do we offer one of the best and most-completely stocked bricks-and-mortar Innova pro shops anywhere, but Mike is also a top rated Ebay seller, and his knowledge and experience with Innova golf discs is what makes this so.

Mike also enjoyed playing in disc golf tournaments and found during the early days that many of the events in California were held in the southern part of the state. This involved a lot of time and travel expense. He first formed the East Bay Disc Golf Club and organized weekly leagues, and then created an annual tournament called "The Caldecott Open," which incorporated the two Bay Area courses at the time, Berkeley Aquatic Park and Moraga Park, both in the East Bay. He named it for the Caldecott Tunnel that connected the two courses. Later Mike, along with another enthusiast, Leonard Muise, developed the concept for the first "NorCal Series," which once in practice included not only the Caldecott Open but also tournaments throughout the Bay Area, in Lakeport and Santa Cruz, in Sacramento and Gold Country. The NorCal series was arguably responsible for an explosion of disc golf in northern California and attracted players from throughout the state.

Because disc golf had become such a big part of our lives, we went into our new life and business adventure not only with the idea of earning a living as innkeepers, but also with the plan of including disc golf. We visualized a property with a course on which we could play, hold tournaments and teach people the game, as well as a pro shop in which to sell discs.

Our desire to build a course had much to do with dictating the location of our venture. Since we needed a minimum of ten acres, very simply, California real estate prices were prohibitive. But we used this to our advantage. For what we sold that 1,300 square-foot starter home in the East Bay hills, we were able to afford a new home, a business and 40 acres in Wisconsin. It was because of a valuable suggestion by Mike's brother, Jeff, and a family history in the Northwoods, that we ultimately landed on the north shore of Squaw Lake at Sandy Point.

The lesson to derive from the condensed version of our story is about two things: First, identifying your passion and then developing a vision that includes or fosters that passion. The trick to achieving a dream life is to apply this passion and vision to a career. This is just another way of saying what Confucius said: "Choose a job you love, and you will never have to work a day in your life."

In Chapter 1: Is This Business For You? I stress the importance of being a "people person," as the first characteristic any aspiring innkeeper should consider. By sharing our story of how we developed the idea of combining our passions and experience to create our business, I attempt to further illustrate the following for you to consider: A successful innkeeper will have a strong sense of home. He or she will have a passion for homemaking, decorating and cleaning, landscaping and gardening. If the inn is a bed-and-breakfast, a passion for cooking, baking and menu planning is essential. The successful innkeeper will be passionate about building and fixing things, and as pointed out in Chapter 7, have the ability to expect the unexpected and weather many different kinds of storms.

Optimism is another personality characteristic that will be helpful to not only innkeepers, but also to all aspiring business owners. It's one thing to have a passion and a vision and quite another to have the confidence to believe you will be successful. Optimism helps, however, it must be peppered with a healthy does of pragmatism . . . or let's just call it realism. For as much as you may hope for dream life, no matter what you create, you cannot avoid reality.

Our reality after we found what we believed was the perfect setting for our dream life—for the world's first disc golf resort—was at times as absurd as a comedic film script. Were the cabins at Sandy Point perfect? No. The reality was all but one had to be rebuilt. And in that process, the constant motion of swinging a hammer and wielding a paintbrush gave Mike a case a carpal tunnel syndrome that required surgery, putting him out of commission for months! We therefore had one of his childhood friends move in with us—a character we called Ivan—who took on handyman chores and kept us entertained. And the disc golf course we built, was it perfect? Certainly not. But as we often say, "it is what it is."

The reality is Sandy Point is a heavily wooded course literally carved out of the property. Golfers with long arms who prefer golf holes without obstacles so that they can capitalize on their ability to regularly throw a driver 300 to 600 feet won't like it.

Is the Northwoods of Wisconsin the perfect place to raise a family? Well, yes. But *for us*, it turned out to be only in the summer. During our first winter, the region experienced record cold temperatures. I recall a two-week period when the thermometer dipped to 40-degrees BELOW zero. It led me to purchase an expensive pair of LaCrosse boots, but unfortunately this was *after* I suffered frostbite on my toes. Mike and I learned to weather the cold with proper gear and limited exposure; however, after Willow was born, the meaning of cold weather translating into what was safe for our baby made us reconsider our desire to be there year round. In addition to the unbearable cold, we didn't know how much we'd miss the company of neighbors once we had children. When summer ended and our resort guests returned home, we were left alone in the woods well outside of town. Gone were all the kids with whom our little girls could play and gone also were all the parents with whom we could commiserate about the strange and often mysterious odyssey that is parenthood.

When Camille came along in 1997, our reality included a move to Tucson, Arizona, where we have spent the past 15 winter seasons. Moving to Tucson was definitely not part of our original life plan or business plan. It's a completely different world in Tucson, especially in regard to climate. Tucson is in the heart of the Sonoran Desert. It's bloody, crazy hot in the summer the way the Northwoods is freakin', crazy freezing in the winter.

And so, we go back-and-forth.

"It's the best of both worlds," people often say. This is, of course, just another way to call it a "dream life." And, yes, our life may appear that way and we certainly feel fortunate to have made it work all these years. But the reality of moving twice per year is challenging, and it's become more complicated as the girls have grown older and have obligations with sports and activities in Tucson. Maintaining two households has been a financial burden as well, and we're now counting dollars along with the years left before we can get back to the original dream of a full time life in the woods. And, well, maybe a low-maintenance condo somewhere in a mild climate to use during the months when it seems that winter just won't end.

Our current goal is to continue living at Sandy Point in the summer and remain in Tucson during the school year until Camille graduates from high school in 2015. If and when the economy stabilizes or improves and if we can avoid any major disasters, we'll fulfill that goal.

Is that optimism or pragmatism? If you answered, "both," then I believe you have what it takes to go after your dream life and live happily-ever-after. Of course, we're still planning on a happily-ever-after scenario, and since we've managed to stay in business for 20 years with our sanity in tact—we consider ourselves successful. It is optimism, however, that continues to play an important role, because another goal we have is to report continued success after 20 more years!

We hope you learn something from reading about our real experience, but you can also learn a thing or two from the silver screen. The films *Dirty Dancing* starring Patrick Swayze and *A Walk on the Moon* starring Diane Lane, for example, are both set at summer vacation resorts. The television series *Newhart* is based at a 200 year-old inn in Vermont, which is run by a couple who left New York City in search of a simpler life and, I believe, solitude for Newhart's character, an author of how-to books. (We writers do need our solitude!) Of course, there's also the old series *Petticoat Junction*, which focuses on life at the "Shady Rest Hotel." These fictitious stories and characters may offer absurd and romanticized notions of an innkeeper's life; however, I contend that the life of an innkeeper is indeed, both romantic and, at times, absurd.

Shortly after we purchased the resort and we were still in California, my brother-in-law, Jeff, sent us a videotape via Federal Express. There was a yellow sticky note attached to it with the message: "Watch this. Pay attention to the resort owners: You in 20 years." The movie was *The Great Outdoors*, starring Dan Aykroyd and John Candy. It's about a Chicago area family that spends a week's vacation in the Northwoods of Wisconsin, and we watch it each time we return to the resort. The crusty resort owners, played by Robert Prosky and Zoaunne Leroy (aged 58 and 53 respectively when the film was released in 1988), own and operate "Wally and Juanita's Perk's Pine Lodge." The original script describes them as "a middle-aged man and a middle-aged woman, asleep in the stuffed chairs in a small office behind the front desk. They're snoring gently. He's in Bermuda shorts, an 'I'VE BEEN TO DULUTH' t-shirt, black knee socks, leather sandals and a Milwaukee Brewer's cap, Juanita is wearing a sundress, peds, cheap jogging shoes and a Budweiser visor." After an initial greeting from a barking German shepherd with a snout full of porcupine quills, the owners rouse from their slumber and waddle to the front desk to greet Chet Ripley (Candy) and his family. Wally and Juanita act first as desk clerks, then as bellhops escorting the group to its cabin, "The Loon's Nest." Handing them the keys, they offer useful information like, "you could get the shits from the well water." Later in the film we see Prosky also act as bartender and host at the resort restaurant, and finally as lifeguard or security patrol when warning of the dangers of keeping the young kids out of the local abandoned mines.

Twenty years down the road, I don't think Mike and I appear quite as crusty as Wally and Juanita—and we definitely have a better wardrobe—but the film does portray a brief, realistic glimpse into the life of Northwoods innkeepers, including dealing with the ludicrous, madcap adventures of some of the guests. By the way, Wally and Juanita may not have been the most attractive role models, but we certainly found them entertaining.

Another example of a film depicting an absurd yet realistic glimpse into the idea of attaining a dream life is the 1988 film *Funny Farm*, starring Chevy Chase and Madolyn Smith as Andy and Elizabeth Farmer. Because we, Mike and Michele, have just a little bit in common with Andy and Elizabeth, this is one of several movies on our list of old favorites. *Funny Farm* is a story about a young couple that moves out of the city to a home in the charming countryside of Vermont. Andy leaves his job as a journalist and plans to write the great American novel. They give up everything and set off to create their dream life in a village called "Redbud," a place they imagine to be straight out of a Norman Rockwell painting. From the onset, everything goes wrong. There are extremes, like a dead body buried in the garden for example, but it's actually a very simple plot: Couple in search of a dream life fails to understand that reality will get in the way.

"We came to Redbud filled with hopes and dreams of a better life," says Andy. "And basically, we've seen those hopes and dreams crushed and battered before our very eyes."

Just like Andy and Elizabeth, Mike and I learned that life doesn't really turn out how we plan it. It turns out the way it does. And sometimes it's even better than we plan. Once you realize and accept this, the music may rise and you'll get your Hollywood happily-ever-after.

As for 20 years from now? If we make it and manage to maintain our life at Sandy Point, we'll most likely resemble Katharine Hepburn and Henry Fonda in the film *On Golden Pond*. I already do a pretty decent loon call.

Chapter 10:
Profound Conclusions

Twenty years later we have no regrets over taking the plunge into the world of innkeeping. As I'm still thinking about Henry Fonda's last film, *On Golden Pond*, which we watch every summer, I recall the scene when the Thayer family celebrates the eightieth birthday of Fonda's character, Norman Thayer Jr. In this loveable curmudgeon's speech over cake and burning candles he claims, "I've been trying all day to draw some profound conclusions about living fourscore years. Haven't thought of anything. Surprised it got here so fast." Then he pulls his wife close and says, "But I'm glad I got to spend so much time with this beautiful woman."

If I were to draw profound conclusions about living a score of years as an innkeeper, like Norman Thayer, they would include not only my surprise at how fast our twentieth anniversary got here, but I'd also have to say that it wouldn't have been as enjoyable without my partner, Mike. I could not have made this business a success without him. This adventure is something we dreamed up together and with a lot of hard work and dedication, together we have enabled it to succeed.

That said, my final piece of advice is to go into this adventure with a partner. And make sure it's a partner you trust *and* love. You'll be spending a lot of time with this person, so it has to be someone who can stand you at your worst as well as at your best. And vice versa. Equally important is that the division of chores matters. Granted, the job requires a multitude of talents; however, it is a rare person who can do it all and do it all well. So, choose a partner who is a good yin to your yang, or perhaps, yang to your yin. In other words, if you've got the brains, finding someone with a bit a brawn could be the key to your success.

Beyond brains and brawn, innkeeping actually requires three key "B-word" characteristics, or what I'll call, "The Three Bs for B-n-Bs or Innkeepers. They are: Brains, Brawn and Beauty.

Innkeepers need the brains it takes to manage and market the business. Knowledge of bookkeeping and budgeting, computer programs, website management and reservations systems are key to a successful and profitable operation. One must be quick-witted in dealing with some of the unexpected things guests may say and quick to act when a key appliance or piece of machinery needs attention or repair.

Some of that machinery often requires heavy lifting. Innkeepers therefore need the brawn to move furniture, appliances, sporting and outdoor equipment. It's an active, physical job. Good health is important.

Finally, by referring to beauty I don't mean to imply you must be a physically attractive person to make this work. You do, however, need to present a beautiful property. The property is your product and no matter how brainy or brawny you are, you must attract guests who are willing to pay to spend their precious vacation time with you where you live. Do you know how often we've had people walk into our office who are looking for a new place to stay because the property they booked online, which they thought would be beautiful, was actually a dump? In 20 years, too many to count. But a far greater number of people have walked into our office and have proclaimed with great enthusiasm how "beautiful" Sandy Point is.

"Wow, this place is beautiful," they say. "You're living a dream life!"

Yes, we are indeed.

Acknowledgments

I dedicate this book to the people responsible for making my life better than any dream life I had imagined, and that's my husband, Mike, and our daughters Willow and Camille. I further acknowledge all the wonderful people who have chosen to make Sandy Point Resort their annual vacation destination. We are blessed to have you in our lives and appreciate your continued support. I especially want to thank Christine Cozzens and Laura Santos Aniballi, who each summer remind me I have the best job in the world.

Many thanks to my biggest supporter, Ric Bollinger, of McKenna Publishing Group. Without your encouragement and daily texts, this book would not have been written. I'd also like to thank Melinda Bollinger, Leslie Parker and Sligo Literary Agency.

Robin Meloy Goldsby, you are my angel. Thank you for the prompt that finally got me going. Anne Tubbs Beaver, thank you for always checking in and keeping me grounded. Jeanine Barlow Ertel, same goes to you, my true friend.

I'd like to thank my innkeeping colleagues, Jenny Gibson, Sue and Denny Robertson, Sue Heil, Jan and Kim Wilson, and Loretta Zortman, as well as all of the members of the Minocqua Area Resorts Association, and Al Hanley, former director of the Minocqua Chamber of Commerce.

In the Wisconsin disc golf community, we are forever grateful to Joe Weinshel, Terry Miller, Johnny Rumble Pecunia, and all the captains of our team tournaments. Rest in peace Steady Ed Headrick and Tim Silenske. We love you and miss you. We'd also like to thank our friends at Innova Discs, especially Harold Duvall, Sam Ferrans, Dave Dunipace, Mark Molnar and Jonathan Poole.

Thanks to Scott "Stu" Cook, aka "Captain Stubing" for all your hard work and dedication to Sandy Point, and to Bryan Nelson for emergency services and construction expertise. Dennis Squires, your help with tournaments and your friendship brings great joy and humor to our dream life. And finally, Robin, you are the hottest and kindest UPS man in the United States and we've loved you for 20 years!"

About the Author

Michele VanOrt Cozzens is a former journalist and newspaper columnist, and author of the column "First Person Plural," originally published in the San Francisco Bay Area. A collection of her columns is included in her book, *The Things I Wish I'd Said*. She and her husband, Mike, have owned and operated Sandy Point Resort and Disc Golf Ranch, the world's first disc golf resort, for 20 years. They are both members of the Professional Disc Golf Association (PDGA).

Michele is the author of five previous books, including the award-winning novel, *A Line Between Friends* and the memoir, *I'm Living Your Dream Life: The Story of a Northwoods Resort Owner*. She is the co-founder of HerBeware, a grassroots effort to educate the public on the potential dangers of unregulated herbs found in dietary supplements. Profits from book sales have gone to both HerBeware and to the Breast Cancer Research Foundation.

Michele currently lives with her husband and daughters, splitting time between the Northwoods of Wisconsin and Tucson, Arizona.

www.michelecozzens.com

Michele Cozzens is available for lectures, readings and book club appearances. For information regarding her availability visit her website or call 888-588-3233. For more information about Sandy Point Resort, visit: www.sandypt.com.

CPSIA information can be obtained
at www.ICGtesting.com
Printed in the USA
FSOW02n2142280916
25535FS

9 781932 172621